SLEEP & GROW HEALTHY

DREAM YOUR WAY TO A HAPPY, HEALTHY LIFE

Tim Simon

First published in 2018 by Grammar Factory Pty Ltd.

© Tim Simon 2018
The moral rights of the author have been asserted

All rights reserved. Except as permitted under the *Australian Copyright Act 1968* (for example, a fair dealing for the purposes of study, research, criticism or review), no part of this book may be reproduced, stored in a retrieval system, communicated or transmitted in any form or by any means without prior written permission.

All enquiries should be made to the author.

 A catalogue record for this book is available from the National Library of Australia

Printed in Australia by McPherson's Printing
Cover design by Designerbility
Editing and book production by Grammar Factory

Disclaimer

The material in this publication is of the nature of general comment only, and does not represent professional advice. It is not intended to provide specific guidance for particular circumstances and it should not be relied on as the basis for any decision to take action or not take action on any matter which it covers. Readers should obtain professional advice where appropriate, before making any such decision. To the maximum extent permitted by law, the author and publisher disclaim all responsibility and liability to any person, arising directly or indirectly from any person taking or not taking action based on the information in this publication.

CONTENTS

Introduction	7
Sleep: the keystone of a healthy life	8
The healthy sleep spiral	10

PART 1: THE WAKE-UP CALL

1. The Problem	19
The stress response	21
Poor sleep as a symptom	28
Poor sleep as a cause	30
2. The Solution	35
What is sleep, anyway?	37
How is your sleep?	45

PART 2: SLEEP AND GROW HEALTHY - THE POSITIVE SLEEP SPIRAL

3. Thinking Well: Forming a Healthy Sleep Mindset	53
Connect sleep to a bigger purpose	56
Challenge limiting beliefs	58
Visualise it!	64

4.	**Working Well: Mastering Work-Sleep Balance**	69
	Set sleep-protecting boundaries	72
	Identify your work stressors	77
	Take back control	80
	Find meaning in your work	83
5.	**Moving Well: The Sleep-Exercise Connection**	87
	Make your move	89
	The right kind of fit	95
	What about pain?	99
6.	**Eating Well: The Ingredients for a Good Night's Sleep**	105
	Why quality is key	106
	Minimising sleep saboteurs	110
	Lose weight, not sleep	112
7.	**Loving Well: The Art of Sleeping Together**	**121**
	Snoring	124
	Incompatible body clocks	132
	Maintaining the love	137

PART 3: STRATEGIES FOR BETTER SLEEP

8.	**Your Sanctuary**	145
	A relaxing environment	146

A supportive bed	152
Buying your mattress	157
9. Your Routine	**161**
Setting your schedule	162
Schedules for shiftworkers	166
Healthy supporting habits	168
10. Your Dream Team	**177**
The traditional route: getting a sleep study	179
Beyond the sleep study: who does what?	180
Choosing the right match for you	185
Taking charge of your team	191
Conclusion	195
About the Author	199
About the Create a Dream Foundation	201
The beginning of Create a Dream	202
Acknowledgements	205
Notes	209

INTRODUCTION

'This year, I'm going to get healthy.'

How many times have you made that promise to yourself? New Year's Eve looms and you perform a life audit, cataloguing all the areas where you're not tracking the way you'd like to be. *This year it's going to be different*, you think. You're going to fix up your eating and lose those extra kilos. You're going to get that beach body and recover faster from those nagging injuries. You're going to get a handle on your work stress and become more productive and successful. You're going to get into a healthy headspace and regulate your emotions. You're going to build stronger, deeper relationships. You're going to be more creative and have more fun!

You know that great all-round health, or wellness, is the key to living your best life. You know that you've got this one body, this one lifetime and this one opportunity to become the person you want to be. Life isn't about surviving – it's about thriving!

But how many times have you collapsed in a heap, halfway through January, worn down already by the overwhelming lists of habits, goals and KPIs you've set yourself in the quest to become healthy? Despite your best efforts, the life you want is eluding you. You're feeling stuck – unfocused, unmotivated and unfulfilled. You know that you're not living the life you want to be living, but you just don't know what to do about it.

What if you could simplify things? What if there was just *one* habit you could work on that, if practised consistently and well, could bring your life into a healthy balance? A habit that could bring you:

- Greater emotional regulation and mental health
- Stronger and deeper relationships
- Healthier appearance and greater attractiveness
- Balanced hormones and healthier body weight
- Faster recovery from illness and injury
- Greater protection against infections, cancers and heart problems
- Better concentration and clearer thinking
- Enhanced productivity and work satisfaction

There is such a habit.

What's more, it's cheap, it's universally accessible and, deep down, you already know how to do it.

Yes, that's right. I'm talking about sleep.

Sleep: the keystone of a healthy life

Can the third of your life that you spend unconscious *really* bring so many benefits? It's a habit – as inevitable as breathing air or drinking water. It's a sometimes welcome, sometimes inconvenient time-filler that marks off one day from another. Sleep is nothing special.

And anyway, you get enough sleep.

Or do you? Chances are, you're one of the vast majority of Australians who struggles to get any decent shut-eye. According to several recent studies of our national sleep habits:

- One in five Australians get less than six hours of sleep a night.[1]
- Almost 75% of us have trouble falling asleep.[2]
- Up to 35% of Australians experience frequent difficulties staying asleep or getting adequate sleep.[3]
- A further 35% of us say we don't feel refreshed when we wake up, and suffer daytime fatigue and irritability.[4]
- Between 4% and 7% of the population are suffering from serious sleep disorders at any one time.[5]

Three-quarters of the population are generally tired and irritable, with over a third of us in chronic sleep debt. And within our already overtired population, we have a subset of people who are so sleep deprived they're basically the walking dead.

Sleep deprivation is no joke, and you know this from experience. Poor sleep casts a deep shadow across your world. Every silver lining becomes a storm cloud. Every molehill becomes a mountain. The black dog moves in and digs holes all over your lawn. The gremlins in your mind get their own radio show. And if this sleep deprivation becomes chronic – well, you can forget about having any success in your life.

If it were just a matter of being tired and irritable, or slowing down your personal growth, the sleep debt issue wouldn't be so urgent. But the more modern scientists dig into the problems associated with ongoing sleep deprivation, the more concerning these statistics become. Poor sleep actually *undermines* your health in some big ways. Depression. Anxiety. Cancer. Heart disease. Obesity. Alzheimer's disease. People who suffer from chronic sleep depletion are far more susceptible to all of these nasties.

If you're worried you've got a bit of sleep debt going on, it's time to wake up and smell the coffee.

The healthy sleep spiral

That's why I've written this book. I know that you have a vision for a healthy, fulfilled life. And I know that you're looking for the best way to get there.

I'm going to show you how fixing your sleep habits will get you to where you want to be. I believe that great sleep is the key to a healthy life and the best way to bring about great social, emotional, physical and spiritual balance. Great sleep will get you out of survival mode and help you to thrive.

Think of all the different parts of your life as connected and moving in a spiral. That spiral is either moving in a positive upward direction, or heading downward in a negative direction. Changes in one area are dynamic and affect other areas, keeping the momentum moving in whichever direction (up or down) you're going.

In this book, I want to put sleep at the centre of that spiral. Instead of relegating it to the last and least important element of your life, it's time to recognise it as an integral part of your habits, actions and activities. If you start making positive changes to your sleep, your habit spiral will move in a positive direction, which in turn will bring greater health and a happier life.

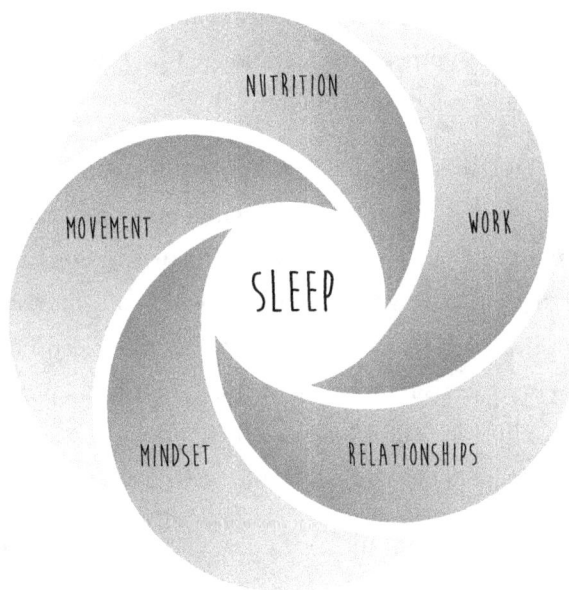

Could you put something else at the centre of that spiral? Yes. I'm not going to claim that sleep is a magic pill – the only habit you ever need pay attention to in your life to bring health, happiness and success.

But sleep is a pretty great place to start. Here's why:

First, sleep is a brilliant diagnostic tool. Because sleep is connected to everything else going on in your life, it can help you interpret your life. If you look honestly at how you're sleeping, it will tell you what you need to know about how you are travelling in your work, your relationships and your health. You might be telling yourself, 'Yes, I'm happy, I'm going great in my work life' – but your sleep patterns could be telling you something different. You might be thinking, 'This new diet is really working well for me' – but your sleep patterns might have another interpretation. How you're sleeping is a window into how you're *really* living.

Second, sleep is a useful focal point. You are bombarded with health and wellness advice. It can be overwhelming to think about all the different areas of your life that you could tweak. Sometimes, you get conflicting pieces of advice. What should you prioritise? Where should you begin? Here's where – sleep! Because sleep impacts all other areas of life, it is the perfect starting point for improving your health and wellbeing. And when it starts improving one area of your life, you'll notice the flow-on effect into other areas.

Third, sleep is a universal tool. Of all the new habits to adopt, getting better sleep has to be one of the most achievable out there. Unlike some expensive health fads, getting better sleep is something everyone can try. It doesn't require special skills or resources. It's low cost, low risk and requires you doing more of something that you already enjoy (and if you don't enjoy it yet, you will).

How do I know all of this? Because I've lived it.

Back in 2010 my own life reached a crisis point. I lost my beautiful mother to cancer, which affected me deeply – especially my sleep. One and a half years later, I was still struggling to sleep well. By this time, the rest of my world was also crashing down around me. My partner of four years and best friend in the world decided to leave me because I couldn't connect to her in the way that she needed me to. I was 25kg overweight. I'd left a successful job in advertising where I'd been top of the pile, and my small importing business was crumbling. I was choosing lots of bad habits. I didn't like how I felt, how I looked or who I was. Everything was spiralling out of control, and something needed to change – I just didn't know what it was.

Most mornings, I'd find myself lying awake at 3am. Unable to get back to sleep, I'd get up and go for long walks along Brighton Beach, thinking about everything that was going wrong and desperately seeking answers.

Finally, I had a vision come to me. For the first time in my life I was truly awake. I started to see the patterns in my own life for what they really were. That epiphany is what drove home to me the crucial place of sleep in my life and sparked my personal journey back to health and happiness. That journey informs every page of this book.

Soon after, I joined my father in the family business, Regal Sleep Solutions. On the ground in the business, day in and day out, I was magnetising people just like me – people whose poor sleep was wreaking havoc in their lives. On the surface, these people were just shopping for a mattress, but underneath I could sense they were looking for something so much deeper: connection, meaning, a reason to get out of bed in the morning.

That's when my passion for the restorative powers of sleep really kicked in. My thinking moved beyond selling comfortable bedding to finding holistic sleep solutions for hurting people. I may not be a trained sleep expert, but since joining Regal in 2012, I've worked with over 2,000 top health professionals from around Australia to develop the right kind of bedding for their clients and patients. And as I've warmed my hands by their fires, I've gained a deeper understanding of why good sleep is integral to our mental, physical and emotional health, and how we can go about getting it! This vision that 'woke me up' for a happy, healthy and, most importantly, fulfilling life was manifesting in front of me, and continues to build momentum to this day.

In this book, I want to share with you all that I've learnt so that you, too, can sleep and grow healthy. This book is not just about mattresses or sleep hygiene habits. Those things have their place, but they're only the cherry on top. I want you delving into sleep deprivation's root causes, not just tinkering around the edge with symptom management. Here's where you're headed:

Part 1: The Wake-Up Call

Why are we all so sleep deprived? Before you fix something, you need to know why it's broke. Chapter 1, *The Problem*, looks at what's behind the modern sleep debt crisis, and chapter 2, *The Solution*, covers what healthy sleep really is and why it's the way back to health.

Part 2: Sleep and Grow Healthy

The point of focusing on sleep is so that you can grow healthy. But the relationship between sleep and your mental, physical and emotional health is not a one-way street. In this central part of the book, we tease apart these chicken-and-egg relationships in chapters on *Thinking Well, Working Well, Moving Well, Eating Well* and *Loving Well.*

Part 3: Strategies for Better Sleep

We are creatures of habit and habitat. Part 3 looks at the supports and systems that will help achieve greater sleep. We look at how to create *Your Sanctuary* and *Your Routine* as well as who to turn to for professional help in your quest for better shut-eye.

Here's what you *won't* find in this book: technical descriptions of exotic sleeping disorders, in-depth discussions of over-the-counter or prescription sleeping pills or any promises to cure your sleep apnea/restless leg syndrome/insomnia. I'm not a sleep scientist. I'm not a doctor – and I'm not a miracle worker. I believe sleep is the miracle worker, and I'm just the guy who wants to reconnect you to its awesome benefits. So while I can't promise perfect sleep to anyone who reads this book, I am convinced that we've all got what it takes to reconnect with our own bodies and minds and start seeing improvements in health and wellbeing. Whether you're sleep deprived a lot, a little or you seriously can't tell, it doesn't matter, there's something in this book for you.

Are you ready to dig deeper into the world of sleep? Let's get going.

PART ONE

THE WAKE-UP CALL

1. THE PROBLEM

Sleep troubles are not a new phenomenon for the human race. Ancient cultures viewed sleep as a bit of a road trip into the spiritual realm, and they turned to gods to assist them on their way. The Egyptians thought sleep involved a nightly journey to the stars, and used opium to ease them on their way if things weren't working so well. The ancient Greeks sought divine help (and a bit of opium) to ease their sleep woes – the god of sleep, Hypnos, is usually pictured holding a poppy flower. Other less heady sleep aids like chamomile and valerian have been around for millennia, along with some crazy remedies like mandrake bark and lettuce juice.[6]

Sleep disturbance is as old as the human race, so you would think that, as a species, we'd be getting better at dealing with it. And yet, we're really underachieving in the sleep evolution department.

Have you ever wondered why you're supposed to spend over a third of your life recharging the batteries when there's so much to do? I know I have. Sometimes I've wished I could function like a crab or a barnacle. These little sea creatures don't need to give over a huge chunk of their existence to being unconscious. They just go into a trance every so often as they drift along the ocean floor.

Well, it turns out that crustaceans can function on periods of trance-like rest because they don't have brains. That's why humans need something more. (If you're a crustacean, you can put this book down now. You don't need sleep.)

Scientists used to believe that human sleep patterns evolved as a survival tactic – something to keep our primitive ancestors out of the way during the dark and dangerous night hours. This belief led to the idea that we more 'evolved' humans can do without so much shut-eye. However, newer theories have brought this into question.

Consider the restorative theory, which demonstrates that our bodies' reparative functions operate mostly (or, in some cases, only) during sleep. This includes things like muscle growth, tissue repair, protein synthesis and growth hormone release.[7] In other words, sleep plays a vital role in body maintenance – it allows the body to get on with its servicing routine; something it's too busy to handle during the day.

Or how about the brain plasticity theory, which argues that sleep plays a role in how our brains learn new information, consolidate memories and recall stored information.[8] In fact, during sleep our brains perform a whole-body flush out, ridding us of toxic waste products. This takes place via the glymphatic system, which operates a huge 60% more efficiently when we're sleeping.[9] In short, if we skimp on sleep, it compromises our brain's ability to perform that flush. (And if you've ever experienced plumbing issues, then you'll know what it's like to be operating with a malfunctioning flush button and not being able to … well, you can see where I'm going with this.)

So unlike some of our ancestors, we now understand the purpose of sleep. We get that it's not just some funky mental trip into outer space or a chance to chat to a deity. We know it's not an indication of laziness and failure but an essential part of our cognitive performance, productivity, physical health, and mental and emotional wellbeing.

And yet, we're worse at it than ever before.

We have more food security, safer shelter and better bedding than at any time in history. We also have more ways to quantify sleep than ever before. We attend sleep laboratories that can stick electrodes to our bodies and measure our brain activity, heart rate, body movement and oxygen levels during sleep. We wear plastic devices around our wrists to track overnight wake-ups and score us on our sleep quality and quantity. And despite it all, we're more tired and grumpy than ever.

Why is this?

The stress response

Human beings have always experienced stress of many kinds – good and bad, imminent and not so immediate. Over thousands of years, our bodies have developed a strong biological response to stress – the 'fight or flight' response. This is a primitive reflex, developed to help you survive and respond quickly to stressors in order to protect your body, either through fighting for survival or fleeing to safety. When a primitive human was under threat from another animal, their brain would kick into action, priming muscles and quickening the pulse to enable fast physical response. At the same time, the brain would shut down non-essential body functions such as the digestive system, the reproductive system and the immune system.

It makes sense to suppress these functions when you're in fight or flight mode. When you're confronted by a sabre-toothed tiger it's not the time for your body to be pouring resources into healing tissues, digesting food or reproducing. No – you want to be running the hell away, and you want all of your body to be on board with that goal.

However, this kind of imminent threat situation seems very foreign to modern humans, particularly those of us who are lucky enough to live in affluent societies where food is abundant, physical threats are rare and life is really not very strenuous. And yet you activate *exactly the same* physiological responses when you are in situations of perceived stress. When your internet connection is on the blink or someone beeps their horn at you or your boss calls you in for a 'private chat', your brain goes into fight or flight mode, suppressing all of the body functions that aren't immediately necessary.

The only problem is that, unlike your primitive forebears, you rarely ever fight *or* flee, which leaves the adrenaline pumping around in your body. You might *feel* like punching the boss, stomping on the malfunctioning modem or ramming into the car next to you, but given that society doesn't generally approve of violence you take a more passive stance. And guess what this means? The anxiety hormones stay in your bloodstream. Rather than releasing built-up stress through physical action, you push down your stress response and its after-effects linger on.

I'm sure you feel that losing an iPhone really isn't as a big a deal as confronting a cheetah, and it seems weird that your body responds to minor irritations as if they were matters of life and death. So why does it do it?

Author of *The SD Protocol*, Dr Wayne Todd, has a helpful way of explaining why. While modern forms of stress are usually more subtle, they're far more numerous and pervasive, leaving us under more constant stress. So along with our failure to appropriately let go of stress, it seems like modern humans experience more kinds of stress, and more frequently, than our forebears. As Dr Todd explains, we're hedged in by a unique cocktail of stressors: physical, chemical and emotional. This is the modern stress triangle.[10]

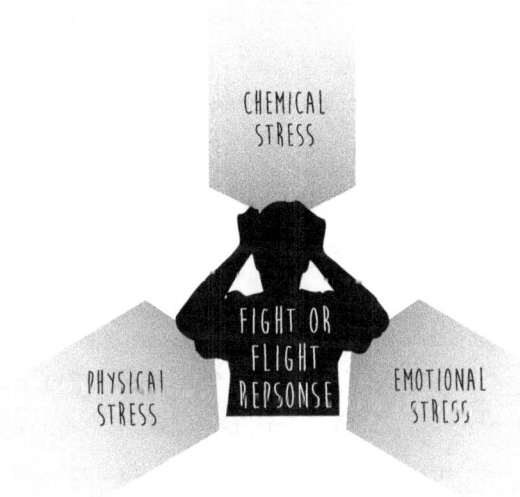

Physical stress

You might think of yourself as having things easy, physically. And it's true – you probably don't have to exert yourself much to find food or perform your daily work. You wear comfortable clothes and shoes and sleep on a comfortable mattress. (If not, we can talk.) Nonetheless, you're under a great deal of physical stress that your body has not adapted to.

Modern lighting is one of the big ones. Before the invention of artificial light, the only source of blue light was the sun. Pre-industrial humans benefitted from exposure to natural blue light during waking hours, and with the sunset, enjoyed a gradual decrease in blue light and the accompanying onset of calm and sleepiness. Hundreds of thousands of years of evolution embedded this natural light pattern into our functioning, resulting in our biological clock, or circadian rhythm – the system responsible for regulating biological processes within a twenty-four-hour cycle.

You, on the other hand, spend your life bathed in a short-wavelength form of light emitted by the sun and electronic devices like laptops, tablets and mobile phones. Today, the average person spends more than seven hours a day immersed in electronic blue light, often well into the hours leading up to bedtime. This type of light heightens alertness and increases reaction time, both of which mimic the stress response. At the same time it suppresses the production of melatonin, which is your body's natural sleep-inducing hormone.

It's not just the light that's problematic; it's the altered postures you find yourself in. Thanks to the kinds of jobs we do, as well as our obsession with technology, modern humans are constantly hunched: heads forward and down, shoulders rounded, chests tightened and brows furrowed. Whether you're in computing, in research, in retail, in hairdressing, in physio or other manual therapies and labours, you most likely spend your days with your arms out in front of you, reaching forward, leaning over or hunching your shoulders for a good part of the day. As Dr Todd points out, these very postures mimic the posture of the stress response and kick off the cycle of muscle priming, adrenaline circulation and systemic suppression of the fight or flight response.

Chemical stress

The next side of the modern stress triangle is chemical stress. The twentieth century brought an explosion of synthetic (human-made) products to the market that have displaced their previous natural counterparts. So much of this advancement in technology has been beneficial for the human race and integral to our progress. Synthetic products are generally stronger, more enduring and often more versatile than their natural counterparts.[11] On the other hand, we're still in the very early stages of interaction with, and adaption to, a whole new world of synthetic inventions, and there are many unknowns. It's all one big experiment.

Here's just one example. For millennia, soap was made from fats and oils, sometimes mixed with ash, clay or sand. Then in the 1930s, a traditional ivory-soap-making company called Procter & Gamble hit upon a formula for synthetic detergents and its production exploded. They released their first detergent in 1933 and their first shampoo shortly after. The formula for their most successful laundry detergent, Tide, was perfected in 1945. This product is widely credited with sinking the traditional soap industry.[12] Now go and take a look around your own household – your bathroom, your laundry, your kitchen. You might buy the 'natural' handwash and the 'organic' detergent, but all of these are synthetic products. These are not products our ancestors were living with, not even 100 years ago!

Now, you or I may not be drinking our laundry detergents or taking heavy chemical concoctions. Nonetheless, our bodies still have to process all the chemicals we come into contact with. Maybe you're using Domestos in the bathroom, or you're spraying Roundup in the garden. Or perhaps you're on the contraceptive pill and taking synthetic hormones into your system, which then need to be metabolised by the liver. Then there's make-up, antiperspirants, aftershave! When chemicals are absorbed through your skin, your body has to work hard to process these foreign substances. On top of all of this, there are the chemicals in industrially produced foods, many of which are genetically modified foods (GMOs).

Right now, it's worth taking a minute to recognise just how widespread these new, synthetic materials and substances are. Almost everything we're using, wearing, eating, working with and even sleeping on has been touched by some kind of chemical that was completely foreign to our species not so long ago. And while we are proving to be adaptable and very hardy creatures, it's not a long bow to draw to realise that the chemical loads we're bearing in our bodies must be putting a whole lot more stress on our systems.

Emotional stress

Along with the physical and chemical stressors we have in our modern society, there's emotional stress. Emotional stress can be caused by past experiences, current situations or anxieties about the future.

What's interesting, though, is that even if life is going well today, your past emotional stress could still be living on in your body if you haven't dealt with it. We all know the idea of carrying emotional baggage – this baggage is how our body stores our memories of trauma. Much of this baggage is a learnt physical response that reactivates when new, current emotional events trigger a similar situation for us. That past stressor could be a bankruptcy, an illness, a death, a divorce or any number of emotionally charged events.

Here's the problem: you may not be aware that your bodily response to threat remains activated even after the threat has vanished. This is because, in situations of emotional trauma, the *idea* of the threat lives on in your mind, and the body will keep reacting with the fight or flight stress response, producing cortisol and keeping your mind on high alert as long as it perceives the threat.

Not only do our brains have this ability to hold onto and relive past threat, we've also developed an amazing capability to anticipate potential danger. This is called anxiety. Anxiety is different from fear. Fear is the emotion you feel in the moment of danger, when you're actually under threat. Anxiety, on the other hand, is the emotional state you are in when you merely *anticipate* this danger. So you're not actually in danger – you may never be in danger – but you have the ability to anticipate it anyway. And quite often, anticipation of a fearful situation is much worse, and lasts much longer, than the actual experience of fear. It's like waiting to go on a roller coaster: the horror of watching the ride take off, hearing people scream and imagining your own fate usually outweighs the fear felt during the ride itself, which starts to ease as soon as you realise you survived the first big dip.

We live in the age of anxiety. Many of us live in a heightened state of arousal much of the time. Add this to the physical and chemical stressors we're under, and it's clear that modern human beings are subject to very high loads of stress.

Poor sleep as a symptom

Sleep is one of the biggest casualties of the modern stress triangle, and most of us are suffering.

This modern stress triangle is what lies beneath your struggle to sleep. Some of us do, of course, experience external sleep disruptors: shiftwork, young children, travel and other interruptions. But for many of us, this poor sleep is related to chronic stress.

When it comes to producing the stress response, the brain doesn't discriminate. Our adrenals increase cortisol production in response to all types of stress – physical, chemical and emotional. And when we're producing high levels of this stress hormone, sleep is inhibited.

This inhibition expresses itself in two ways: sleep deprivation and insomnia.

Sleep deprivation is the absence of adequate sleep, usually caused by either personal action (staying up late to watch TV, setting an early alarm for a shift) or an external factor (neighbourhood noise, wakeful children or a snoring spouse). It's when you *could* be asleep but you aren't due to external factors that potentially can be controlled.

Insomnia, besides being the title of a terrifying Stephen King novel, has a very broad definition. It's an umbrella term for a collection of related sleep disorders, all characterised by a difficulty falling or staying asleep. This is the situation where you *could* be asleep, you *want* to be asleep and the environment is conducive to sleep, but you just can't sleep.

There are three overarching types of insomnia, though it's not unusual to suffer from a combination of the three. These are:

- Sleep-onset insomnia, where you have trouble falling asleep at the beginning of the night.
- Sleep-maintenance insomnia, where you have trouble staying asleep throughout the night.
- Early-awakening insomnia, where – you guessed it – you wake up much earlier than intended and have trouble getting back to sleep.

These types of insomnia generally come down to one overarching internal factor: the hyper-arousal of the nervous system. As Dr Wayne Todd says, 'Insomnia is not a disease in and of itself. It is a symptom of something else going wrong. Think of it as a light on the dashboard of your car, telling you there is something going on under the hood that needs attention.'[13]

Poor sleep then feeds the cycle, because when our bodies don't have time to heal themselves, remove waste products, regulate hormones and deal with inflammation, the whole stress response just gets worse. The parasympathetic nervous system continues to suppress the functions in our bodies that allow for rest, digestion, reproduction and repair. Our flight or fight response remains switched on.

Poor sleep as a cause

The tricky thing about poor sleep is that, while it starts as a *symptom* of too much stress, it then feeds back into a negative health loop and becomes a *cause* in itself.

Take a look at the following list of problems that flow from inadequate sleep.

Weight gain

Diet and exercise are the usual suspects to target when it comes to the problem of obesity. But what about sleep? Did you know that poor sleep mucks with the hormones that regulate your hunger signals? That's right – it decreases leptin, which regulates how much food you feel like eating, and adds insult to injury by increasing ghrelin, which stimulates the body's fat production and makes us reach for the foods more likely to help with fat storage. So the less we sleep, the more likely we are to feel hungry and to reach for the high-fat, high-carbohydrate foods to compensate for our tiredness.

Then there's the link to type 2 diabetes. When the brain doesn't get sufficient downtime, it increases secretion of the stress hormone cortisol, which makes it harder for insulin to do its job. This in turn means that too much glucose stays in the bloodstream, and then insulin resistance comes along and suddenly there's a party on your midsection and every fat cell is invited (BYO flotation device). And while everyone is off blaming the refined sugars, there's a great deal of evidence that sleep deprivation is part of the cause, not just the effect, of the pre-diabetic insulin-resistant state.[14]

High blood pressure

What do you think are the most important factors for good heart health? Most people would say that a healthy diet, regular exercise schedule and smoke-free lifestyle about cover it. That's mostly correct, but here's a fascinating fact: regardless of your weight, smoking and exercise habits, and even your age, people who sleep less than six hours per night are about twice as likely to die of a heart attack or stroke.

Sleep apnea, a serious condition where breathing during sleep is obstructed, has long been acknowledged to cause high blood pressure, arrhythmia, stroke and heart failure. But evidence is mounting that *anyone* who experiences fragmented sleep and gets less than six hours a night is at higher risk of these cardiovascular troubles.

Neurological impairment

Researchers have long been puzzling about the link between poor sleep and neurodegenerative diseases like Alzheimer's and Parkinson's disease. We know there's a strong correlation between sleep loss and these illnesses, but for a long time we didn't know why. Though the exact mechanisms are far from clear, recent research has shed a lot of light on this relationship. It goes back to the glymphatic system I was talking about before, which has the important role of removing a protein called amyloid beta from the brain. This protein accumulates in people with Alzheimer's, and recent studies suggest that patients who sleep fewer hours or have more disrupted sleep have higher concentrations of this waste product.[15]

Mood disorders

All of this bad news about sleep is probably getting you down. Well, you may as well stay there, because poor sleep and depression go hand in hand. When you don't get enough sleep, your brain's ability to regulate your emotions drops significantly. Sleep-deprived people are more likely to misinterpret neutral stimuli (such as facial expressions or tones of voice) as negative or threatening, tend to be moody and reactive, and generally feel sad or down.

Based on brain-imaging scans, researchers suspect that this occurs because links between the parts of your brain that should regulate emotion go haywire when you don't sleep enough. The amygdala, a part of the deep brain that functions as our emotional control centre, becomes overreactive, and the hippocampus, which processes positive or neutral information, starts underfunctioning. So poor sleep drains your happiness, literally.

Low productivity

It's probably obvious already that selling yourself short on sleep doesn't accomplish much. While we continue to fool ourselves into staying up late to finish that project, crunch those numbers or (cough) write that book, the fact is that we're both producing substandard work at the time *and* undercutting our productivity for the next few days. Forget the sleep hacks, take off your 'sleep is failure' t-shirt and put down that energy drink. Sleep deprivation makes you dumber. Working when you're tired causes you to be less creative, less witty and more prone to making mistakes.

And it's having an impact on our work and economy. A 2011 Deloitte Access Economics report found that the total cost associated with sleep disorders in Australia was $36.4 billion, while a more recent study put the true cost at closer to $66 billion each year.[16] In the USA, some companies have taken this productivity issue so seriously that they're paying staff to sleep![17] It's catching on in Australia, too. When I visited Google headquarters in Sydney I got to see their room full of sleep pods, which they encourage employees to use as necessary throughout the day. When top businesses are pouring resources into sleep, you know how important it is.

Accidents

While we're thinking about being unproductive, there's nothing quite as unproductive as injuring yourself out of a job. Unfortunately, sleep is once again the culprit for quite a number of workplace injuries and accidents. This is unsurprising, as someone with eighteen hours' sleep deprivation has the same kind of reflex response and mental acuity as a driver with a 0.05% blood alcohol reading. This is really alarming when you think about it. Plenty of people are sensible enough not to drink and drive, yet may pose as much of a danger at their workplace simply through being sleep deprived. The research on this topic suggests that sleep problems sit beneath about nine per cent of workplace injuries. And in the last year alone, Australia lost 394 adults to vehicle or workplace accidents where the primary cause was falling asleep.[18]

So we've got weight issues, heart issues and brain issues. We're moody, unproductive and sometimes downright dangerous. It's the stuff of nightmares ... if only we stayed asleep long enough to have any.

What can be done?

2. THE SOLUTION

After all that talk of chronic stress and its nasty sidekicks, you're probably ready to go on a month-long holiday. Clearly the only solution to this depressing downward spiral of stress, bad sleep and poor health is to avoid all stress.

Options for avoiding all stress in the modern world are slim on the ground. Here's a good one: join the Amish. Communities in this American religious sect have kept themselves out of modern-day madness by retaining a nineteenth-century agrarian lifestyle. The most secluded old-order Amish communities have no electricity in their homes, no telephones, and rely on horse and buggy for transport. And it's working for their stress levels. A health survey of women in these communities reports that Amish women weigh less on average than their mainstream counterparts. They also take fewer prescription drugs, hold lower rates of mental illness and perceive their own lives to be less stressful.[19]

If joining the Amish sounds like a good solution to you, then what are you waiting for? Put down this book and buy yourself a one-way ticket to Pennsylvania! (BYO butter churn.)

For the rest of us, let's acknowledge that it's not possible to escape modern life for a stress-free existence. But we still need time for rest and repair to get a break from the fast pace of life and to stress-proof ourselves to survive, even thrive, in its midst. Say, a good chunk of time to lie down and put our feet up. In the dark. On something comfortable. With our eyes closed.

Reclaiming your sleep is the most practical solution to stress-proofing your life. Sleep is the ultimate escape from reality – and you can do it without having to leave your own home. And unlike an awkwardly challenging yoga pose, it's something your body is innately capable of doing.

Here's what healthy sleep can bring you:

1. **Vitality and longevity.** Sleep has countless health benefits: managing weight, restoring memory, reducing inflammation, spurring creativity, improving athletic ability, and even warding off depression. Getting adequate sleep, both quantity and quality, also increases our odds of living longer.[20]

2. **Intelligence.** Do you remember that old saying 'sleeping on a problem'? Study after study has proved that after a good sleep, our ability to process and solve complex problems and perform tasks increases by tenfold. We all know that great sleep means we can concentrate and absorb ideas better during the day, but the evidence is mounting that sleep-time itself is where all the magic acquisition and consolidation of knowledge happens!

3. **Good looks.** Okay, so now I'm getting a bit shallow. But beauty sleep is a real thing! Some of this is due to all the health benefits we've already noted, and a healthy person is going to look their best. But it's also psychological. A number of studies have shown that well-rested people are perceived as far more attractive than their sleep-deprived counterparts.[21] No wonder my partner, Juliana, is always taking naps!

Good looks, intelligence, vitality ... what's not to love about sleep?

Even better, you have an inbuilt drive to get this kind of sleep. Your body needs the right balance of wakefulness and sleep over a twenty-four-hour period. This is called sleep/wake homeostasis. Like hunger and thirst, which are cues that your energy or hydration levels are getting low, feeling sleepy is the cue that you need sleep. Tiredness and yawning are not signs of moral failure but of your body's desire for something it needs. But like your other bodily drives, you may have become disconnected from this cue. Both external and internal stressors have caused you to ignore, misread or override your body's drive for sleep/wake homeostasis. You may have stopped recognising its signals, or the signals themselves may have become warped and broken.

The rest of this book is all about rediscovering your natural desire for sleep and your amazing ability to sleep well. It's about clearing away the mental, emotional and physical clutter that is impeding your sleep drive and your ability to recognise or respond to its cues. First though, let's dig a bit deeper into what sleeping well really means, and get you to evaluate where your own sleep is at.

What is sleep, anyway?

Do you really need to know what goes on during sleep in order to do it right? Sleep should be simple. It's all about non-effort. It's an act of not-doing and un-trying. Isn't the whole point that, if you're doing it right, you won't be awake to notice?

Yet understanding a bit more about what happens during sleep can make a world of difference. For many people, there's a big gap between their perception of sleep (what they think they're doing overnight) and their sleep reality (what they're actually doing). This mismatch drives a lot of misunderstanding and anxiety. When you understand more of what's really going on in your brain and body overnight, you can start to relax and cooperate with your sleep patterns.

Healthy sleep is made up of several different elements: when your sleep occurs, how much of it you get and how effectual it is.

Sleep timing

Every life form on earth, all the way down to bacteria, has a circadian rhythm – a series of physical, mental and behavioural changes that approximately follows a twenty-four-hour cycle. Your appetite, energy levels, body temperature and many other basic functions work according to this schedule.

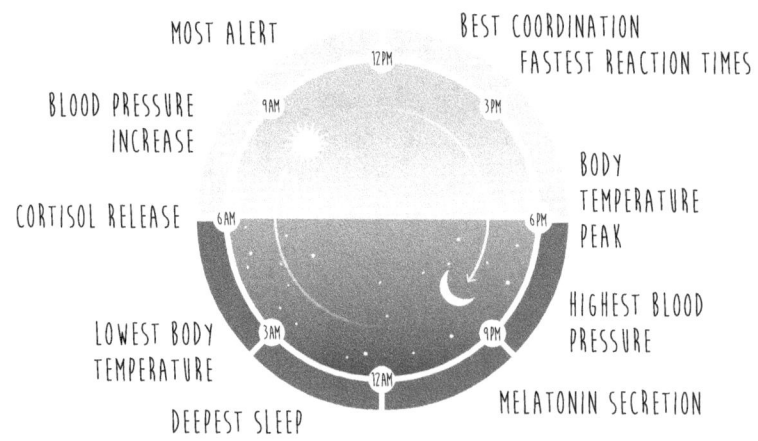

The circadian clock

Our circadian rhythms are largely governed by light. For most of human existence, the main light signals humans have responded and conformed to have been the sunrise and sunset. Our bodies, just like everything else in nature, are set up to work in harmony with this cycle.

As I write, the 2017 Nobel Prize for medicine has just been awarded to three biologists for their ground-breaking study of the master genes that control the human body's circadian rhythms.[23] Their work has helped show why we humans suffer so much when there's a temporary mismatch between our external environment and our internal body clock, like when we travel across time zones and get jet lag. On my business trips to China, for example, I've often felt so unsettled and out of whack that I've struggled to connect to the people I'm there to see – so much so that I now ensure an extra day between long-haul flights and business meetings. However, it's not just a matter of feeling a bit vague or having a bad business outcome: these scientists have also shown that chronic misalignment between our lifestyle and our internal rhythm can contribute to many illnesses and diseases.

To complicate things, however, each of us has a different circadian rhythm. If you've lived much of your life quietly amazed at people who can function before noon and fall asleep before midnight, you may belong to a relatively small category of people known as 'night owls'. Night owls – like my fiancée, Juliana – tend to naturally stay up late into the night, sleep in, and feel most alert and energetic in the afternoon and evening. 'Larks', on the other hand, like to go to bed in the early evening, get up early, and feel most alert in the morning. I'm a lark.

The majority of people are neither a night owl nor lark. The percentage of people in each category varies by study, but the general estimate is that around 10–15% of people are night owls, 20–30% are larks, and 55–70% of people are in between the two. But if you're trying to fit your sleeping habits around other people or life happenings and not tuning into your own sleep rhythm (or 'chronotype', as the sleep scientists call it), you may unwittingly be doing yourself out of the healthy sleep you need.

Some research suggests that your chronotype can affect more than when you feel most energetic – there seem to be some actual behavioural differences between the types. For instance, night owls are more likely to smoke, drink alcohol, and be less physically active. They're also more likely to be addicted to coffee and sugar. It's possible that much of this is an attempt to ease the stress of being a late-night person living in an early-riser's world.[24] Interestingly, night owls may also be more intelligent, contrary to the folk wisdom that says early to bed and early to rise makes one … well, you know the rest.

The upshot? Healthy sleep should fall in line with your circadian rhythm, which will follow a roughly twenty-four-hour cycle – but the best time for you to sleep within that cycle will depend on your chronotype.

Sleep quantity

The amount of sleep you need is a hotly contested topic in some circles. Sleep historians have uncovered all kinds of interesting sleeping patterns in different times and cultures, including sleeping in two shifts. Medieval monks, for example, used to break their sleep into two parts, getting up for an hour of prayer in the middle (yawn!). Their less virtuous counterparts (who sound very much like the people I knew during my not-so-professional poker phase) would break sleep to visit the neighbours, gamble and smoke tobacco.[25]

Sleeping in one chunk overnight may well be a modern phenomenon, but we're modern humans. We face modern stressors. And for that reason, we need to listen to modern research and expert recommendations. After putting the hard word on eighteen different sleep experts and conducting wide-ranging research, the National Sleep Foundation in the USA produced the following guidelines in 2015:[26]

Age	Hours recommended	May be appropriate	Not recommended
Newborns 0-3 months	14-17	11-13 18-19	Less than 11 More than 19
Infants 4-11 months	12-15	10-11 16-18	Less than 10 More than 18
Toddlers 1-2 years	11-14	9-10 15-16	Less than 9 More than 16
Preschoolers 3-5 years	10-13	8-9 14	Less than 8 More than 14
School-age children 6-13 years	9-11	7-8 12	Less than 7 More than 12
Teenagers 14-17 years	8-10	7 11	Less than 7 More than 11
Young adults 18-25 years	7-9	6 10-11	Less than 6 More than 11
Adults 26-64 years	7-9	6 10	Less than 6 More than 10
Older adults ≥65 years	7-8	5-6 9	Less than 5 More than 9

Most of you reading this book will fall into the 7–9 or 7–8 hour sleep-need categories. (If you're an infant, congratulations on your reading skills. Now get back to bed!) We should all be aiming to carve out something around eight hours a night.

A caveat: sleep needs do differ. More is not necessarily better: in fact, research indicates that those who sleep more than nine and a half hours at night die younger! Dr Chris Winter, American neurologist and sleep expert, writes in his book *The Sleep Solution*, 'If you sleep well, feel well, and don't have any symptoms of excessive sleepiness, whatever amount of sleep you're getting is probably okay.'[27]

But be honest with yourself. A lot of people who think they are doing fine on below-average sleep are fooling themselves. I was chatting to my operations manager, Pete, about his sleep routine, and he was boasting about only needing five or six hours. But then he admitted to feeling tired! I told him he was no Elon Musk and got him to stop drinking coffee at 8pm – and he's now getting an extra hour a night. If you're sacrificing sleep to save the world or invent something amazing, it's possibly worth it. But if you're sacrificing sleep for more time surfing the internet, you're doing your body a disservice.

In the end, quality is going to trump quantity when it comes to getting the most out of your sleep. So let's move onto that 'sleep well' bit …

Sleep quality

Sleep quality is harder to get your head around than sleep quantity. You can spend the correct amount of time in bed, but because you can't observe yourself it's hard to know what actually goes on during those hours, and whether you're getting 'the right kind' of sleep. What's more, your sleep perception (what you think you're doing during the night) and your sleep reality (what you're actually doing) are notoriously misaligned, as many sleep studies show.[28]

Many people don't realise that healthy sleep is not one big downtime. Instead, we have a rollercoaster of lighter and deeper sleep across the night. You typically experience three to five cycles of sleep each night. During each cycle we go through several stages of sleep, each of which has its own special function. There are two basic types of sleep: Rapid Eye Movement (REM) sleep and everything else! Different models break these down further, into four, five or even six stages, but I'm going to keep it simple and give you just three types of sleep. (Otherwise you'll be here all night, and that's not my aim.)

First, there's light sleep. This is a state you have to pass through between being awake and deep sleep, or deep sleep and dream sleep. It typically makes up the bulk of your sleep. During light sleep, eye movement stops, heart rate slows, body temperature decreases and you can be easily awakened. It's the one you fall into when you're at a boring movie, drooling onto your shirt before your date nudges you and you explain that you were 'just resting your eyes'.

Then there's deep sleep. Deep sleep is slow-wave sleep in which your body builds energy for the next day, stimulates growth and development, repairs muscles and tissues and boosts your immune system. Deep sleep is essential for waking up energised and refreshed and helps maintain general health. It's very hard to be roused from slow-wave sleep. Inevitably, your spouse, child or pet will try to get your attention the moment you have fallen into slow-wave sleep.

Finally, there's dream sleep, usually called REM sleep. This final sleep stage plays a key role in learning and memory. It is thought to be important for consolidating and processing emotional memories (sensations of happiness, joy, fear and so on) as well as procedural memories (such as how to tie your shoelaces). During REM sleep your brain also replenishes the feel-good hormones that boost your mood during the day. Your body will often twitch during REM, and your special other may accuse you of trying out your new disco moves in your sleep. Feign ignorance.

In each sleep cycle, you move through light sleep and deep sleep into REM, but the proportions of each shifts throughout the night. Between these cycles, brief awakenings are a very normal part of a night's sleep. In your earlier cycles you spend more time in deep sleep, whereas the later cycles (in the early morning hours) contain mostly light sleep and REM. This explains why we're often more easily roused in the early hours (like the notorious 3am wake-up), and also why we're told that every hour of sleep we get before midnight is worth double the hours we get after. Note for night owls: this is less about the actual time of sleep, and more about the fact that our earlier hours of sleep are the most restorative due to their higher proportion of deep sleep.

This overview of sleep stages should help bring some perspective on what quality sleep looks like. The journey through Sleepy-Time is not on a flat road through a monotonous landscape, but on a windy road through a varied terrain. Brief waking spells and changes in position don't mean your sleep wasn't any good – they might just represent your moves through the different stages. Some people get so worried about sleeping too lightly during the morning hours that they get themselves in a tangle. This is called 'sleep state misperception' or 'paradoxical insomnia', although its older, cooler name is 'twilight sleep'.[29] (I tried to grab Kristen Stewart for an in-depth interview – she declined.) Now you know what counts as 'normal sleep', you should be able to avoid giving yourself paradoxical insomnia.

How is your sleep?

After all of that, it's time to stop, take stock of your own sleep habits and have a think about how healthy your sleep is.

There are lots of complex ways to profile your own sleep, but here I want to keep things simple. The idea is to get a picture of your basic sleep habits and do an assessment about how healthy your sleep is.

At this point, let's talk about wearable sleep trackers. If you use any kind of app or wearable device to track your sleep, congratulations on prioritising one of the most fundamental parts of your health!

However, tread with caution around these devices. For one thing, they don't track sleep in the same way a sleep lab would. They are motion sensors, which track physical movement, not polysomnographs, which track electrical activity in your brain and map patterns of activity to identify different stages of sleep. So, while these sensors might be able to tell whether or not you're asleep, how much you move is not a reliable indicator of what sleep stage you're in.[30]

So while you might love data, I suggest you put aside the expensive sleep monitor for now. Don't get paralysis by analysis. The key marker of quality sleep is the ability to fall asleep, and to get back to sleep, within a reasonable time. And the way to test whether you're doing that well is old-fashioned and cheap: it's tuning in to your own body. How alert and well-rested do you feel on a regular basis? That's the best clue.

If you're someone who hasn't put much thought into sleep before now, answering these questions will help bring some awareness to your habits and patterns. You can take that awareness forward into the rest of the book as you use the sleep key to bring some order, health and sanity back to your own life. I have recommended this survey for use in many of the health professional clinics I've worked with across Australia.

Exercise: Assess your sleep

SLEEP TIMING

In the evening, I usually start feeling tired at:
I usually go to bed at:
On weekdays, I wake up at:
On weekends, I wake up at:
I feel my best when I go to bed at:
I feel my best when I get up at:

SLEEP QUANTITY

On a 'good night', how many hours do I spend in bed?

How many nights a week do I count as a 'good night'?

What's the latest I have been to bed in the last few weeks?

What's the earliest I have been to bed in the last few weeks?

SLEEP QUALITY

The amount of time that I usually take to fall asleep is:

The number of times that I usually wake up during the night is:

If I wake it is usually due to:

> Internal factors (my own snoring, nightmares, the call of nature)
> External factors (e.g. children, noises, a snoring partner)

If I wake up during the night, the time it usually takes for me to fall asleep again is:

How rested do I feel upon waking in the morning?

How alert do I feel during the daytime?

PRIMARY SLEEP CONCERN

When I have sleep issues, it's usually most likely to be:

☐ Help, I can't sleep!
☐ Help, I'm always sleepy!

Now that you're more clued into what healthy sleep actually means, and you know where you stand with your sleep timing, quantity and quality, you're ready to start looking at the rest of your life in order to get yourself into awesome, healthy sleep habits.

Just a heads-up: the harder stuff to solve is around sleep *quality*. Sleep timing and sleep quantity you can generally solve with a bit of discipline, but quality requires a bit of digging and poking around in the deeper, darker parts of your being. We're going to start in the most powerful place of all: your mind.

PART TWO

SLEEP AND GROW HEALTHY — THE POSITIVE SLEEP SPIRAL

3. THINKING WELL: FORMING A HEALTHY SLEEP MINDSET

Now that you know that stress is your problem, and stress-proofing your life through better sleep is the solution, you're ready to look at the key areas of your life and make some changes to get into a positive sleep spiral. Before you spring straight into action, however, there's something you need to do.

You need to get your subconscious mind on board.

Have you ever had the experience of setting yourself a goal and then finding yourself acting almost in opposition to that goal? Maybe you've decided on a new early-morning gym routine, but then find yourself sleeping through your alarm every single day. Or you've decided to cut down on sugar, but somehow you keep stocking the pantry with all your old favourites and gravitating to social situations where you feel forced to eat dessert. It's like there's one part of you that's really sold on your new goal, and another part that's trying to sabotage you.

I had an experience of this just recently. I was listening to a podcast where Richard Branson explained how he limits his alcohol intake to only a few times a year. As someone who really enjoys a drink but sometimes overindulges, I was impressed that one of my business idols was really prioritising his health.

I decided to imitate Branson's approach to cut down my own drinking. I learnt how Branson avoids social awkwardness during functions by filling a champagne glass with something exotic but soft, like cranberry juice and soda. The very next weekend, I tried to implement my new strategy – but my subconscious had other ideas! I found myself doing the exact opposite. I found myself ordering an alcoholic cider instead of a coffee – at 10am in the morning! The next day I ordered a cocktail instead of a healthy smoothie. I was devastated. What was this overt self-sabotage? I felt like there was an internal tug-of-war happening.

Well, that's exactly what is happening when the subconscious mind is not yet invested in the goal. You see, beliefs reside at both the conscious and subconscious levels of our minds. Your conscious beliefs are influenced most by reason and evidence, and you can change them through education and awareness. Your subconscious beliefs are far less rational – they are deep-seated assumptions, shaped through your life experiences and your interpretations of those experiences. Social psychologist Jonathan Haidt describes the relationship between the two as like an elephant and its rider. The small rider is like the rational conscious brain, while the elephant represents the primitive, sensory-driven part of the brain.[31]

And when your conscious and subconscious are in conflict, then the subconscious is going to win. Your subconscious mind asserts far more influence on the amygdala (that little part of the brain that plays a primary role in our decision-making and emotional reactions) than your conscious mind does. In fact, it has up to 95% of the control. Just as a rider can't control a stampeding elephant by sheer force, you can't change your habits by sheer force.

What's more, the sabotaging behaviour of your subconscious is going to be reinforced, because your brain delivers the reward drug, dopamine, each time it perceives progress towards your subconscious goal.[32] This leaves you in a pattern of trying a new habit, failing, and then beating yourself up for what you think is a lack of discipline or willpower, when what is really happening is that you are achieving, and rewarding yourself, for the subconscious goal instead!

For a few people, fixing up sleep habits will be mostly a matter of conscious education and persuasion. That could be you. Maybe your subconscious is hanging out for some good sleep, but you've simply been ignorant about the damage that burning the candle at both ends is doing to you. Now that you realise sleep is vital to your health, sanity, intelligence and even your attractiveness, you know it's time to change your ways.

For most of you, however, just as I did with the alcohol issue, you'll experience some resistance – whether to sleep itself, or to some of the surrounding web of habits that impact on your sleep. In your case, you need to train the elephant!

Changing your subconscious beliefs is possible. The idea that we can positively reprogram ourselves is the basis of hypnosis, neuro-linguistic programming, Cognitive Behavioural Therapy and many other psychotherapeutic techniques. But you don't necessarily need to book yourself in to see a psychologist yet. There are also some simple techniques you can use on your own. To change your subconscious mind, you just need to learn to speak its language. Unlike your rational and education-loving conscious mind, your subconscious responds most directly to ideas that appeal to the imagination and the senses, not the intellect. To woo your subconscious you want to connect sleep to your greater purpose, remove any limiting beliefs and visualise success. You're going to learn how to do those things next.

Connect sleep to a bigger purpose

Getting clear on *why* you want to do something is key to making any lasting life changes. If you have a clear, overarching purpose in life, one that you're attuned to both consciously and subconsciously, then tying your sleep habits into that purpose will make your motivations rock solid and give you the drive you need to adopt healthy sleep patterns. So to change your sleep, you need to have a clear purpose.

My own life coach, Dr Ben Carvosso, has driven this home to me during our sessions together. Ben sees many people whose overarching purpose is not clear, and whose motivations are often negative. 'So often, people do what they feel obligated or pressured do,' Ben says. 'They have someone that "shoulds" them: you should earn more money; you should get a better job; you should get healthier; you should lose weight. If they do what they should do, without any positive driving force behind it, without deciding who they need to be, they never succeed.'

But if you have a clear and compelling purpose, Ben says, then it's like jumping in a river. 'The river is flowing. When you're in your mission, when you're in your purpose, it's like you're in a river being pulled along. It's not necessarily easy, but there is an ease to it – an ease to making the decisions about moving forward. Then, with grace, gratitude and courage, you move forward.'

After reading the first few chapters of this book, you're probably already 'shoulding' yourself about sleep: 'I should start getting to bed earlier...'. But 'I should get more sleep' is not a compelling life purpose. Changing yourself for the sake of appearance, or out of obligation, is not going to have long-term effects. External drivers like this are lousy motivators and won't cut it with your subconscious mind.

Instead, try finding an internal motivator – a greater purpose – that you can link to your sleep.

To find your purpose, ask yourself:

- Who is it you really want to be?
- How do you really want to feel in your life?
- What is your purpose?
- What are your values?
- Where does good sleep and great health fit in?
- How will better sleep serve your purpose?
- How does better sleep express your values?

Back to my 10am cocktails experience. 'Drink less because Richard Branson does' was clearly not enough of a motivator to get me to change my drinking behaviour easily. I needed to connect it with my own values and purpose. My five core values are love, family, leadership, growth and passion, and these help me live out my purpose. The first thing I needed to do with the drinking issue was to feel and know for myself how more moderate drinking would serve these values. I want to drink less to be a better version of *me*, not to be a poor Richard Branson imitation.

Connecting sleep to a bigger purpose will be most helpful to you if your sleep is of a lower quality due to poor lifestyle or health, or a lack of respect for the role sleep plays in your life. In this situation, getting better sleep will require a shift in priorities and some changes to the web of habits that could be interrupting your sleep – things like use of technology, poor diet or bad work boundaries, all of which we'll look at in future chapters.

But what if sleep is a huge priority to you, and you desperately want it, but you can't seem to get it? What if you do prioritise sleep, but it's still eluding you? Then it's time to go a bit deeper.

Challenge limiting beliefs

What stories do you tell yourself about your ability to sleep?

In the previous chapter I asked you to categorise your main sleep problem as either 'Help, I can't get to sleep', or 'Help, I'm always sleepy'. Generally your main sleep issues will fall into one of those two camps, and you'll label yourself accordingly. You're either struggling with falling asleep but are staying asleep, or you go to sleep okay but never feel refreshed.

Limiting beliefs about sleep form the backbone of the problem called 'insomnia'. Insomnia, at its core, is when someone *believes* they're not sleeping or that they can't sleep. Someone struggling with insomnia may indeed have a big sleep debt – or, paradoxically, they may actually be getting enough sleep, but just feeling terrible and anxious about their sleep quality or their inability to get to sleep. According to neurologist and sleep guru Dr Chris Winter, anxiety and fear are at the bottom of most cases of insomnia, and for the insomniac the inability to sleep becomes part of the identity.[33]

Unsurprisingly, people with insomnia have more negative beliefs about sleep than people who sleep well. However, a ground-breaking study from Canada has shown that by doing nothing other than working to remove those negative beliefs, and replacing them with more positive ones, researchers were able to dramatically improve the sleep of the participants.[34] In fact, Cognitive Behavioural Therapy, which teaches people how to identify and deal with irrational beliefs, is now the most effective cure for insomnia.[35]

Do you have limiting beliefs about sleep?

I'm often on the shop floor with customers discussing their sleep issues and helping them find the right bedding. These encounters can get quite personal as people open up about their poor sleep situations. So I've heard it all when it comes to people's beliefs about sleep!

Some people have identity-based beliefs: *I'm a poor sleeper – I've never slept well. I haven't slept in years.*

Some people reveal beliefs about the need to stay in control: *I don't need sleep. Sleep is for the weak. I've got too much to do, sleep just doesn't fit in – I've got other priorities.*

Some people hold beliefs rooted in fear: *I'm a light sleeper. I need to listen out for my kids. I can't switch off.*

Some people reveal beliefs that want to keep them a victim: *It's not my fault I can't sleep. My work is to blame … My family is to blame … The dog is to blame … It's not in my control.* (I have one friend who blames the magpies!)

And some people just don't think they deserve to feel good. They have almost an allergic reaction to the idea that they are allowed to feel refreshed and well-rested and enjoy their life.

All of these are limiting beliefs – ideas about yourself that are holding you back in your habits and behaviours and preventing you from enjoying healthy sleep.

Do any of them ring a bell for you?

When I looked at my limiting beliefs around changing my drinking habits, I realised that I was telling myself a story of childhood deprivation. I struggled with weight as a child and my mum therefore wouldn't keep chocolate or lollies in the house. My stepmother used to keep some at her home, however, so whenever I went there I just gorged myself. I didn't know how to handle the abundance; it's like I was stocking up for the future, knowing I would be deprived again once I returned to my mother's house. I think the same thing happened with the alcohol. My subconscious mind heard, 'There's going to be an absence and it could be a long one, so you'd better stock up on the drinks right now!'

I didn't trust myself that I could have a drink if I really wanted to. To get past this, I needed to work on my limiting beliefs around deprivation.

The same thing can happen when you try to change your sleep habits. What exactly is holding you back?

> **Exercise: Identify your limiting beliefs**
>
> Your beliefs about sleep could be centred on sleep routines and habits. Or they could be centred on your ability or inability to fall asleep, to stay asleep or to get good depth and quality of sleep.
>
> What limiting beliefs might you hold about sleep? Do this *Why?* exercise to drill down into what could be holding you back in your sleep habits. Start with the problem you most relate to:
>
> > I can't fall asleep easily. *Why?*
> > or I need medication to help me sleep. *Why?*
> > or I can't stay asleep throughout the night. *Why?*
> > or I can't wake feeling refreshed. *Why?*
>
> Once you've hit on your first answer, keep asking why and see what comes up.
>
> For example:
>
> > I can't stay asleep throughout the night ... because I'm a light sleeper.
> > I'm a light sleeper because ... I was a light sleeper as a child.

> I was a light sleeper as a child because ... I didn't feel safe.
>
> I didn't feel safe because ...?
>
> Keep asking 'why?' until you have exhausted your ideas. It doesn't matter if nothing super clear reveals itself – you've made a good start towards awareness just by asking the question.

Once you know more about your subconscious attitudes towards getting healthy, you can assess whether these attitudes or beliefs are serving you.

1. Acknowledge that beliefs are not truths

This is often the hardest step. Your internalised beliefs are so powerful that they have directed your choices and actions for so long. It's not too strong a claim to say that your beliefs define your reality.

You will be tempted to validate your beliefs. As Evelyn Waugh wrote, 'When we argue for our limitations, we get to keep them.' A good trick here is to imagine what life will be like in five, ten or thirty years from now if you continue down the same path with these beliefs.

2. Let go of your need for that belief

Louise Hay, author of *You Can Heal Your Life*, suggests that we often have a need for self-sabotaging behaviours.[36] There's some deeper purpose your beliefs are serving, even if it's an unhelpful purpose. Many unhelpful habits are trying to protect us in some way: procrastination is a way to avoid failure by ensuring we never complete a task; being overweight is often a way to emotionally protect against potential rejection.

What purpose might your poor sleep be serving? What need is it filling? And are you willing to let it go?

You might not be able to untangle exactly what need your poor sleep habits are filling. It doesn't matter. The first step is simply being willing to let go of that need. Say, 'I am willing to release my need for … taking too long to go to sleep/waking frequently/being unable to go back to sleep.'

3. Try on some new beliefs through affirmation

Positive affirmations are a great way to change your internal belief soundtrack. They include statements like:

- Sleep is a natural process and my body knows how to do it.
- I am becoming someone who drifts off to sleep with ease.
- More and more, I can relax into a deep and gentle sleep.
- When I awake at night, I can quickly and easily fall back to sleep.
- I can leave my work and go to bed, trusting that everything can wait until tomorrow.
- I awake in the morning feeling well-rested and alert.

To be effective, an affirmation should be:

1. Focused on the present, not the distant future.
2. Focused on the positive, not the negative.

3. Realistic enough to be in harmony with – or at least not directly contradictory to – your present reality.

So don't go with something like 'I am going to stop being an insomniac', and don't jump straight to 'I am the sleep champion of the universe' either. Go for something that gives you a sense of positivity and possibility.

> **Exercise: Create your sleep affirmations**
>
> Write down a few affirmations that will help to shift your limiting beliefs about sleep.
>
> To implant these affirmations into your subconscious mind, you need to repeat them to yourself regularly. You could try saying them out aloud to yourself in the shower, repeating them in your mind as you brush your teeth at night, or writing them down over and over in a journal just before bedtime.

Visualise it!

So you've aligned your goal for better sleep with your higher purpose, and you've worked at shifting some of the limiting beliefs that could cause resistance to your goal.

Now it's time to really employ your imagination – through visualisation.

Visualising simply means giving yourself a mental picture of what you want to achieve. It engages the imagination through pictures. If you can't imagine something, you won't be able to achieve it no matter how hard you work. When it comes to the subconscious mind, imagination trumps willpower. It usually trumps logic and common sense, too. That's why visualisation is such a powerful tool.

How does it work? Brain imagery research has shown that your neurons interpret what you imagine in the same way that they interpret what you actually experience in real life. When you visualise moving your left foot, for example, this use of imagination switches on the same parts of the brain that would be activated when actually moving your foot. Imagining something therefore primes your body to act in the way you've just imagined. This is precisely why visualisation techniques are so popular now among elite athletes.

But sleep is a much less technical, apparently more passive activity than something highly skilled like tennis or playing the violin. So can imagining being a 'great sleeper' really work?

Yes it can! In fact, the great thing about sleep is that it is *not* a highly specialised skill. It's an innate one. Somewhere deep in your brain, you know how to sleep well. Visualisation may just help you reconnect to that 'inner sleeper' that's been buried under a pile of bad habits or too many limiting thoughts.

You can use visualisation in several ways to help your sleep improve. First, you can use it to help you with the act of sleep itself. Sleep-inducement visualisation has long been used to help people chill out enough to go to sleep, and there are hundreds of exercises available in books and on the web to help you. Some of these engage imagined scenarios, like picturing yourself floating down the river on a raft, while others focus on body-scan relaxations. However, using your own imagination to picture yourself simply falling asleep can work just as well: if you can imagine it, you can do it!

> *Your body lets you know when it's tired with a gentle yawn. You lie down in your soft, inviting bed, allowing your weight to sink onto the supportive surface of your mattress. In your dark room, your eyelids close gently and your breathing begins to slow. You can feel the rhythmic rise and fall of your ribcage soothing and calming you. As your mind winds down, your thoughts drift past like clouds. You let them come and go easily as you fall into a deep, restful sleep...*

Don't you feel more relaxed and sleepy just reading that paragraph?

Visualisation can also help you imagine how great your life is going to be when you're sleeping consistently well. Imagine the calm, healthful person you have become. Picture the benefits that are overflowing into your work life, your relationships, your physical health and your passions.

The more detailed and sustained your visualisation, the stronger the emotional link will be and the more convinced your subconscious will become that you are a natural, deep sleeper.

Exercise: Visualise deep, restful sleep

1. Using pen and paper, write down a description of yourself as a natural deep sleeper. Write in the present tense, giving as much detail as possible.

   What are your sleep habits?

> How great does sleep feel to you? How easy is it for you to fall asleep and stay asleep?
>
> How do you feel when you wake up?
>
> 2. Imagine what your life will look like now that you're sleeping so well. What benefits have flowed over into the rest of your life?
>
>   Who have you become?
>
>   Where are you in your life?
>
>   What are you doing?
>
>   What can you now achieve?
>
>   How has your life changed?
>
>   How do you feel?
>
> 3. Return to this visualisation regularly to keep the vision in the forefront of your mind.

If you've had a go at some of those exercises, well done. You've made a great start to taming that elephant. With rider and elephant, your conscious and subconscious minds, heading in the same direction together, it's going to be a much smoother ride towards great sleep.

4. WORKING WELL: MASTERING WORK-SLEEP BALANCE

Thomas Edison is best known as the inventor of the incandescent light bulb, but we could equally label him the guy who killed the circadian clock. The driving motivation behind Edison's remarkable invention was his desire to liberate people from the burden of sleep, which he viewed as a waste of time and productivity. Edison himself averaged twenty-hour work days, reducing this to an 'easy' fifteen hours in his fifties.[37] Artificial light allowed him not only to feed his own workaholic tendencies but to foist them on others: he demanded that workers at his Menlo Park laboratory and in his factories put in long hours, and reputedly interviewed prospective employees at 4am. There's no doubt about it – for the sake of work, Edison murdered sleep.[38]

We live in a sleep-machismo culture, where productivity, success and leadership are associated with burning the midnight oil. You may have noticed that Donald Trump has been getting some bad press about (among other things) his sleep schedule. The current leader of the free world has boasted about getting by on minimal hours, asking the *Daily News*: 'How does somebody that's sleeping twelve and fourteen hours a day compete with someone that's sleeping three or four?'

There's no doubt that this approach is a train wreck waiting to happen. Experts agree that even one hour less sleep than you need, let alone three or four, can seriously affect your decision-making skills, and not for the better. Multiple studies have directly examined the link between sleep deprivation and leadership skills. A major finding is that sleep-deprived leaders are far less inspiring and believable.[39] People reliably rate under-slept speakers as less charismatic, even when the text of the speech is exactly the same, suggesting that fatigue affects your ability to speak convincingly.

However, there's a lot more than speech-giving at risk. Sleep affects your ability to read other people's emotions accurately, as well as regulate your own. Imagine dealing with an employee or a client while wrestling with a severely hampered ability to read and respond to social cues. That's exactly what's happening when you go to work without getting enough rest.

Let's break this down to the neuroscience. The part of your brain that allows you to perform complex tasks, like managing a group of people or staying on top of a long to-do list, is the neocortex – in particular, the prefrontal cortex. The neocortex is the most recent development in the evolution of our brains, and the first to take a hit when you don't get enough sleep. While other parts of your brain, like the evolutionarily older visual and motor cortexes, also suffer from sleep deprivation, higher-order brain functions or 'executive functions' suffer to a much greater degree. That makes sense, since it's in your body's best interest to remember how to breathe and see over preserving your executive functions, but it's still bad news for those of us concerned with organisational leadership.

In my work and travels I've had the chance to meet many impressive, high-flying business executives and smart, savvy entrepreneurs. And I'll be honest – the people I admire most are not those who wear sleep deprivation like a badge of honour. Most of the time those who boast about sleeping only four hours a night are paying for it with poor health and even poorer leadership skills. These people are 'stressers', constantly carrying the burden and worry of their work with them, and working long and hard because they don't want to relinquish any control. They're often not fun to work for or be around.

The ones I admire most are those who are at ease enough to put their work aside, set boundaries and sleep well. These people are what I call 'masters'. A master does not stay up way too late at night, being a control freak or worrying about work. A master prioritises their own bedtime because they are at ease. They have put in place the right mental approach to work and habits that allow them to down tools at a good hour and protect their healthy sleeping patterns.

Unlike a stresser, a master rarely wakes overnight either. A master sleeps right through the night, because they've already got things in place to deal with anticipated problems or issues. They've got a meeting scheduled the next day with the person who's playing the game at a higher level. They've got the strategy lined up for dealing with work concerns.

Those who master themselves at work can relax at night and get better sleep. And because they've slept well, they work well. They've got that virtuous spiral going.

Whether you lead or manage other people in your day-to-day work or are just trying to manage yourself, great sleep is key to working well. But here's the rub: when it comes to your poor sleep habits, it could well be that workplace stress itself is the main culprit. So you need good sleep to work well, and you need to de-stress your working habits in order to sleep well.

What is your sleep telling you about your approach to work? Do you sacrifice sleep to stay on top of things? Do you send emails after hours, respond to texts overnight or check your phone first thing in the morning? If you wake up during the night, how likely is it that work is on your mind? I have been guilty of all of these things and I can tell you, hand on my heart, that it's been to my detriment.

Do you want to be a stresser or a master? Getting yourself into that virtuous spiral starts with setting healthy, sleep-protecting boundaries.

Set sleep-protecting boundaries

We're living in the Information Age. The digital revolution of the mid twentieth-century shifted the focus from industrial production to information technology. Of course we still have industrially produced goods and physical commodities, but information is now the biggest commodity we deal with, and technology is how it's delivered.

Work has no doubt always been stressful for humans, but the Information Age brings with it some unique challenges that add to workplace stress.

First, there's a pressure to be constantly productive. Many of us deal in the commodity of 'knowledge work', a limitless resource that can therefore be produced constantly. Gone are many of the jobs that work to rhythms and seasons: even schools and universities are moving away from the traditional yearly schedules by offering third semesters, intensives and ongoing online courses.

Second, there's a pressure to be constantly available. With the rapid developments in technology we've seen over the last few decades, we now have much more flexibility, freedom and even creativity in where, when and how we engage in work. On the down side, we're always 'connected'. Our phones are by our sides, our fingers at the ready to respond to calls, emails and social media comments. What's more, we're operating in a globalised economy that requires our attention 24/7. As Tony Crabbe expresses it, we're living in an infinite world that combines both no end of possibilities and no escape from them.[40]

Third, there's the pressure that comes from being shackled to technology. We've covered this ground already, but here's a reminder: the average person spends more than seven hours a day immersed in electronic blue light, which alters our circadian rhythms by suppressing melatonin production. With this comes the physical stress of hunching over our devices, and the mental strain that comes from being bombarded with constant information.

How can you counteract these pressures?

1. Switch off

The best and simplest way to nip work stress in the bud and protect your sleep is to place firm boundaries around your use of technology.

The fear of being without your mobile device now has a name: nomophobia.[41] The term, short for 'no-mobile-phone-phobia', describes the feeling of anxiety that around 60% of people feel when they don't have their phone on hand, or charged, at all times. The researchers who coined the term found that nomophobes' stress levels were comparable to wedding day jitters or – my ultimate fear – a trip to the dentist![42]

Turning off your electronics – phone, computer, pager – and making yourself uncontactable for certain hours of the day can take a great deal of effort. But the benefits far outweigh the cost.

Switching off sends a clear message to people that you're a master. It demonstrates to the world, your family and friends and, just as importantly, yourself, that you give priority to your own needs for relaxation, privacy and rest. It reminds everyone that the world can spin without you. This will help your own sympathetic nervous system relax, reversing the physical effects of too much technology and allowing you to get better sleep.

What could this look like for you? It could mean:
- Turning off your phone over dinner
- Leaving your laptop at the office at the end of the day

- Allowing yourself to check emails up until 8pm, then switching off
- Putting the phone on silent overnight
- Keeping all devices out of the bedroom

Some people even go so far as to have a 'Tech Sabbath', when they avoid electronics for a whole day or stretch of time over the weekend. In 'On the Seventh Day, We Unplug: How and Why to Take a Tech Sabbath', Brett and Kate McKay go through all of the benefits of getting your brain off the (electronic) gear for a chunk of time each week.[43] These include breaking the dependency habit, reconnecting with our senses and employing underused parts of the brain. I haven't committed fully to this idea yet, but I'm committed to trying it.

Even if you're someone who is on call, or otherwise required to have your phone or computer on hand for much of the day and night, small steps towards unplugging can go a long way to reducing the overstimulation, hyper-vigilance and stress that could be disrupting your sleep. Abstaining from texting and social media for an hour on the weekend, leaving your phone behind when you go to the gym, or switching over to 'sleep mode' just half an hour earlier on work nights could make a world of difference.

I used to call myself '24/7 Tim', until my dear friend James taught me that to be too available lowers your personal value. Since he drove this home to me, I've started to set firm boundaries – for example, my phone goes onto silent mode from 8pm to 7am. I render myself uncontactable (unless I choose otherwise).

A note for leaders and managers: if you're trying to stay available at all times for your team, you're doing it wrong! If you're needed that much, you're not promoting true leadership in your role. You should be recreating yourself by allowing those around you to handle responsibilities themselves. If you're always 'on' and available, how can other people step up? I encourage the leaders in my team to make themselves dispensable, to hand on responsibilities to others and to delegate themselves out of a role. A true leader will prioritise sleep – starting with switching off.

2. Set a worry hour

Sometimes the boundaries you need to set are not with other people but with your own mind.

We're all going to come across times when we are under pressure and need to spend some time troubleshooting work problems. But what masters have figured out is that it's best to do this in advance, rather than waiting for the worry load to catch up with you. As one of my friends put it to me once, 'Worry about your work at 3pm, not 3am.' It's all about the art of anticipation. In real life, things are going to come up that are stressful and unpleasant. Carving out time for troubleshooting simply means that you've got a better chance of sorting through them so that they don't become an ongoing source of stress that will keep you up, or wake you up, at night.

Have you ever heard of Worry Time? It's a technique used by psychologists to help people with anxiety get on top of their racing thoughts, but it's also a helpful technique for reducing general stress response. Here's how it works:

1. Set yourself a time of day and a time limit (say, half an hour at 3pm).
2. As worries pop into your head during the day, write them down on a list.
3. At Worry Time, set a timer and get worrying!
4. Sort your list into short-term and long-term concerns.
5. Deal with the short-term ones first, writing down any strategies that come to mind.
6. Then give time for the long-term ones.
7. Allow yourself to fret, as it's useless to repress feelings of stress.
8. Write down solutions or strategies as they come to you.
9. If an issue needs more worry time, keep it on the list for tomorrow!

This technique may seem silly, but it can really work. It helps to sort out the big issues from the small so they're not all getting mixed up. It provides space to gain perspective and look for solutions. It allows time to feel fear and stress and let some of it dissipate. And best of all, it will help to calm your mind so you can sleep. I challenge you to try it.

Identify your work stressors

Boundaries are a great start to being a master in the workplace. However, just switching off your phone and learning to limit your worries will not deal with all forms of workplace stress.

We all suffer from work-related stress. Whether it's caused by overwork, underwork, lack of autonomy, harassment, perceived discrimination, job insecurity, tight deadlines, pressure from superiors, lack of resources or annoying colleagues, stress of one sort or another is bound to catch up with all of us at some point. Some of us are in emotionally demanding work: psychologists, therapists, teachers. Others are in physically or mentally demanding high-stakes careers: firefighters, soldiers, doctors, nurses, air traffic controllers. Some of us operate in demanding workplace cultures: commission-based jobs, sales, places where there's ethical pressure. And all of us can experience the general frustrations of day-to-day work: interpersonal conflict, frustrating red tape or paperwork, even plain old boredom.

I don't know what kind of work you do and where you do it. Perhaps you're a nurse, working night shifts. Or you might be an office worker, chained to the desk from 8am to 7pm. Maybe you're a sales rep who is out and about in the car, or a small business owner who works at home, or a health professional who works early mornings and late evenings. But while pressures may vary, most work concerns span occupations. One group of researchers in the United States has identified the four broad categories of workplace stress across both 'blue collar' and 'white collar' occupations:[44]

- Task demands (occupation, careers, workload, job insecurity)
- Role demands (role conflict and ambiguity)
- Physical demands (temperature, lighting, workplace design)
- Interpersonal demands (personality conflicts, leadership style, group pressures)

In your own work situation there will be physical, chemical and emotional stressors that come into play. And while your mind sees these stressors as different, your primitive brain interprets these stressors the same way. They are all perceived as threat, and the stress response flips on: 'Regardless of what causes the stress, the body manifests a similar physiological response: taxing your heart, wearing out your blood vessels, irritating your digestive tract, exhausting your adrenal glands, weakening your immune system, and stressing your pancreas.'[45]

And of course, this heightened stress response is the very thing that cuts into your sleep.

We can all expect a bad day at work now and then. That's life, and it's nothing to freak out about. It's patterns of chronic stress we need to worry about. If workplace stress is ongoing, then it's going to be undermining your sleep quality for sure.

Awareness is the first step. I recommend using the following exercise as a kind of 'workplace stress audit' to get a handle on what your main sources of stress are likely to be.

Exercise: Assess your workplace stressors

1. Think about what your workplace is like and where the stress points might be for you. Write down your thoughts under the following categories:

   - **Task demands:** What is your workload like? What about your work patterns? Do you get too much or too little stimulation and challenge? Do you have accesses to development and resources?

   - **Role demands:** Do you understand your role within your team or organisation? Is there conflict within your role/s? How secure is your job? How much say do you have in the way you work?

> - **Physical demands:** What is your work environment like? Are there physical or chemical stressors inherent in your job? How are the temperature, lighting and workplace design?
>
> - **Interpersonal demands:** Is there effective communication and cooperation in the workplace? Is there quality guidance and support?
>
> 2. Which of these demands are the greatest sources of stress for you? Identify your top five stressors, and write them down.

So you have a list of your top five workplace stressors.

What can you do about them? Does identifying these help you feel empowered now to go and make some changes in the workplace?

Or are you feeling *more* stressed because you don't think you can do anything to change your situation?

Now we're getting to the heart of workplace stress: lack of control.

Take back control

Time and time again, regardless of the particular stressor, it is the underlying feeling of powerlessness, helplessness or 'being stuck' that is actually causing the stress reaction. The same group of researchers who identified the four different stress categories we just looked at found that the foremost cause of workplace stress is 'lack of employee decision latitude' – that is, a perceived or actual lack of autonomy in decision-making.[46] (The second highest cause was uncertainty, and the third highest was poorly managed conflict.)

In fact, many definitions of workplace stress focus on this issue of control. Here's a definition from an occupational health and safety website: '[workplace stress] is the harmful physical and emotional response that can happen when there is a conflict between job demands on the employee and the amount of control an employee has over meeting these demands.'[47]

But here's a further interesting thing about lack of control. Much of it has to do with perception. When you *perceive* that you have no control, you start to stress. When you feel like you have no control, you stop taking responsibility for things.

Linking this back to sleep: it's easy to blame poor sleeping habits on external circumstances. You might say, for instance, that you're going to bed late all this week because of a deadline. Or it's your mean boss, your workload, your physical work set-up that's waking you up in the night. But none of these things is literally keeping you awake. Your boss is not standing over you, propping matchsticks under your eyelids. Your written report with a deadline is not beating you over the head while you try to fall back to sleep at 3am. No – it's your own brain, tick-tick-ticking away, staying too vigilant to let you take the time you need to nurture yourself, relax and sleep. And the only person who has the power to take back control of your monkey mind is you.

This has less to do with where you sit in the work pecking order than you might think, and more to do with perception and attitude. It's about becoming a master in your own workplace role.

The antidote to feeling helpless is to identify small, actionable steps you can take yourself. This increases what is called 'self-efficacy': your positive beliefs about your own ability to exercise influence over events that affect you. Self-efficacy is empowering. If you can take even the tiniest of steps to improve your own situation, whether by making a small external change to your environment or circumstances or changing your own attitude towards a situation, then you will gain more self-belief. This in itself will reduce your stress response, even if your situation does not change dramatically.[48]

Taking steps for yourself does not necessarily mean doing everything yourself. In fact, it will probably mean asking for help.

Exercise: Become the master in your workplace role

Go back to your top five stressors. Now it's time to make a list of action points for each stressor. Ask yourself the following questions to help make a plan for reducing your work stress.

1. **What can I do myself to change this problem?**

   What are some steps you can take to make changes to your situation? These can be internal (about attitude change) or external (changing your environment). It doesn't matter how small they are.

2. **Whose help do I need?**

   Do you need to ask for an occupational health and safety assessment to address your physical set-up? Can you have a meeting with your supervisor to discuss your workload or role ambiguities? Do you need to find a mentor? Do you need HR to help mediate a challenging relationship with a co-worker?

> **3. How can I replicate myself?**
>
> Do you need to hand over responsibilities to other people? Do you need to step back and allow other people to step up? Are there opportunities for delegation?

Find meaning in your work

If, after doing some good work on setting boundaries, identifying your stressors and taking control, you are still experiencing a lot of poor sleep and stress, you may be wondering whether it's time to reconsider the role you're in. Perhaps it's time for you to find a new, more fulfilling career. Work that fulfils more of a sense of purpose in your life and meshes with your values will bring the possibility of better health and better sleep with it.

Working day in, day out in a role you resent or one that goes against your ethics will heighten your risk of chronic stress response. Life coach Ben Carvosso points out that many of us sacrifice our values at work to get certain needs met – needs like certainty, achievement and a sense of belonging. Yet if the work doesn't align with our deeper values, it won't be truly fulfilling. This brings with it an element of discomfort and stress.

But what does it mean to have fulfilling work? Is a dream job one that pays heaps of money? Is it one that eliminates stress?

The organisation *80,000hours.org* has conducted one of the most thorough reviews of all studies about work satisfaction and the ideal job. It concludes, surprisingly, that dream jobs are not the ones that earn the most money. Yes, some money can make you happier, but only a little – and the increase in life satisfaction peters out at a surprisingly low income of $73,000 dollars (AUD).[49] Also surprising, the organisation has discovered that aiming for an absence of stress is not the pathway to fulfilment. A role that is too undemanding can create as much stress as one where the demands exceed your abilities.

The bottom line, according to this organisation, is to look for:

1. Work you're good at, and
2. Work that helps others.[50]

These are the key criteria of what makes a dream job: mastery of your tasks and meaning in what you do. Underneath this, you will also benefit from supportive conditions, supportive colleagues, a lack of major negatives like unfair pay, and work that fits your personal life – but mastery and meaning come first.

After working successfully in the world of sports advertising, I didn't exactly consider a move into mattresses my 'dream job'. Yet seven years ago, when the call came from my father asking for my help to turn around the struggling family business, I saw that it was a perfect fit for my top core values: family and love. As soon as I realised this, I was all in. I wanted to dedicate myself to the family legacy and to the growth of this business, which would help the people I love and give my work meaning. As my role within the business grew, I saw that I was doing work I was good at and drawing on my other core values: leadership, growth and passion. In my role I get to use my skills *and* help people. It's an amazing privilege.

Are you in your dream job? Are you using your skills? Are they being used to improve the lives of other people?

Maybe you've read all of this and think you must move on: your work neither engages your skills nor helps others in a meaningful way. If that's you, perhaps it really is time to seek out something new for the sake of your own health.

But you might be beginning to see some new possibilities in your current workplace. Just asking yourself these questions might open your eyes to the potentials of the work role you're already in. They could give you a new sense of purpose and satisfaction in your workplace. Quite often people are not in the wrong role at all – they're in the wrong headspace. And when the headspace improves, the work does too.

Let me tell you about Lenny, a base maker in our mattress factory. Lenny came to us through an agency placement. He'd had some kind of personal trouble and this funded scheme helped him find a work placement. Lenny started at the bottom of the mattress production chain, where everyone starts, doing 'hog ringing', which involves stapling a felt pad onto the border wire.

Some people would look down their noses at this menial work. But from day one, Lenny embraced his role. He was thrilled to have a new opportunity and he performed his tasks cheerfully and consistently. Despite living a long way from the factory and having to catch public transport, Lenny was never late to work and his hard-work ethic boosted the factory morale. After a few months, Lenny became a gluer, gluing together the foam layers that make up the mattress.

He did that successfully for many years, and now he upholsters our bed bases. Lenny has been with us for eleven years now, and it's a joy to have him in our team.

Does Lenny sleep well? You bet he does. And you will too as you learn to set good boundaries, take back control and embrace a sense of purpose in your own working life.

5. MOVING WELL: THE SLEEP-EXERCISE CONNECTION

It was 2006, and the Socceroos were getting ready to play their qualifying match for the World Cup. But there was a problem. The team was coming off a gruelling stretch of travel, flying in from South America only a few days before the big game. So how did they prepare? If they were like many of us, they'd be pushing last-minute training, nutrition and supplementation. Instead, the team brought in Professor Leon Lack, sleep psychologist, to help them out. Lack worked with the team doctor to create a sleeping and light-exposure plan for the players, and the team went on to win the qualifier in a penalty shoot-out held together by goalie Mark Schwarzer. According to Professor Lack, Schwarzer was, of all the players, the most conscientious about keeping to Lack's protocol. Sleep had saved the day![51]

It used to be that diet, exercise and supplements were the only considerations in the world of optimal sports performance. Now, professional athletes and sporting teams are hiring sleep experts. Real Madrid forward Cristiano Ronaldo receives regular sleep guidance from a sleep coach in order to keep his edge, while the National Basketball Association in America employs a Harvard sleep specialist to help players up their game.[52] As Ariana Huffington points out, for professional athletes 'sleep is not about spirituality, work-life balance, or even health and wellbeing; it's all about performance.'[53]

Sleep is vital, not just for muscle adaption and recovery, but also for the concentration and mental quickness sportspeople need to thrive in high-pressure situations.

And as a performance enhancer, sleep works. One study looked at the sleep patterns of a team of basketball players at Stanford University. Before the study took place, players were averaging 6.5 hours of sleep per night. The researchers conducting the study took some performance stats from these athletes, then placed them all on a seven-week 'sleep extension protocol', stretching the players to 8.5 hours per night. When the stats were taken at the conclusion of the protocol, the team free-throw shooting was up by 9%, their three-point shots were up by 9.2% and they had shaved almost one second off their average sprint times. Their moods even improved![54]

This is great news for elite athletes. But what about the rest of us?

You might not be playing for our country, winning marathons or slam-dunking in front of thousands any time soon, but it's still vital to get the sleep-exercise spiral moving in a positive direction. Sleep gives you the energy to stay in shape and move well in life. And moving well – the right kind of movement at the right time – plays a key role in regulating your sleep. What's more, the exercise-and-sleep combination is one of the most effective ways to combat chronic pain conditions and stop them from holding you back in life.

Do you want to learn more? Let's get moving.

Make your move

Does the word 'exercise' make you feel like hugging the nearest treadmill, or does the very thought make you want to poke your eye out with a bicycle spoke?

If your reaction is a negative one, I'm not shocked. For many, exercise is a form of torture. We 'do some exercise' to work off a big meal or to burn that fat from our midriffs. Our hunter-gatherer ancestors ran out of necessity, whether to chase a meal or to avoid becoming one. Our more recent predecessors stayed physically active down through the centuries thanks to nomadic lifestyles, subsistence farming, hard labour, military training and the occasional weird sport like caber tossing. Today, in the age of motorised transport, domestic automation and industrialised food production, we do exercise on spin bikes that don't go anywhere – and then wonder what we're doing with our lives.

Here's a fact: we weren't born to 'do exercise' in forty-five-minute slots. But we *were* born to move. As Jason Smith, physiotherapist and founder of the Back in Motion health group, likes to say, we were created to be in motion.[55] If you're not moving in some way, shape or form, you're not really living life the way you're designed to live it. Your body is capable of functioning effectively to meet the demands of everyday life. Moving well means embracing a range of activities so that you can adapt to and perform the movements you want, and need, to do every day: bending, reaching, hauling, squatting, running, climbing and carrying. Note: 'pressing button on remote control' is not one of those necessary movements!

The maxim 'move it or lose it' is overused, but it's true. Lack of movement can begin a negative spiral of pain and dysfunction. In Jason's words, 'any joint that doesn't bend, any muscle that doesn't stretch, any nerve that doesn't have connectivity – it's only a matter of time and it will cease to function the way it was intended.' Enjoying physical movement and feeling physically capable is part of what it is to be human, even if our sedentary modern culture has tried to suck that idea right out of us.

Moving well brings with it loads of mental and emotional benefits. It increases serotonin production, which is your body's own natural antidepressant. It increases cognitive function, meaning you'll learn better and remember more. I personally love the sense of mastery I feel when I've grown in my physical capabilities. I love the lift it brings to my mood and the way it sharpens my thinking. When I'm moving well, feeling fit and looking good, I approach life with drive and purpose, and my physical confidence overflows into my workplace and my relationships.

And of course, consistent movement is a crucial aspect of getting a good night's sleep. A study published in the *Journal of Clinical Sleep Medicine* found that patients with primary insomnia had a radical improvement in sleep quality when they added a consistent exercise regimen.[56] They saw:

- A 55% improvement in sleep onset latency,
- A 30% decrease in total wake time,
- An 18% increase in total sleep time, and
- A 13% increase in sleep efficiency.

In a nutshell, participants fell asleep faster, woke less frequently, slept for longer and experienced better quality sleep.

Are you moving enough?

It's all very well for me to mock exercise classes like Spin or Zumba, but it has its place. In our sedentary culture, we all need to be creative and deliberate about cramming in more movement, and whatever form it comes in is all right with me!

If you aren't used to moving much and are worried about the time and commitment involved, don't freak out. According to the Australian Government's health guidelines, undertaking a recommended minimum of 150 minutes of moderate-intensity activity or seventy-five minutes of vigorous exercise per week will help you:

- Reduce the risk of, or better manage, diseases such as cardiovascular disease, type 2 diabetes and some cancers,
- Maintain or improve blood pressure, cholesterol and blood sugar levels,
- Prevent and manage mental health problems, and
- Build stronger muscles and bones and assist in weight regulation.

That's a great list of benefits, and for relatively little investment: just five thirty-minute sessions of moderate exercise a week can do all of that, or three twenty-five-minute sessions at a higher intensity. What's more, you can undertake exercise in smaller chunks throughout the day – say, in ten-minute increments – and it will still give you many of the same benefits as doing it in one bigger chunk.[57]

There are three broad types of exertion activities, and each one of them has particular benefits.

1. **Endurance:** aerobic activities like brisk walking, jogging, dancing or gardening. These activities increase your breathing and heart rate. They keep your heart, lungs, and circulatory system healthy and improve your overall fitness. Building your endurance makes it easier to carry out many of your everyday activities.

2. **Strength:** resistance movements using body weight, free weights or gym equipment. These movements make your muscles and bones stronger, which is especially important as you start aging and losing muscle tissue. Resistance training will not only help you carry out functional tasks day to day, but it will help you look trim and speed up your metabolism (because the more muscle mass you have, the more energy your body needs to burn!).

3. **Flexibility:** exercises like Tai Chi, Pilates, some forms of yoga and stretching. These movements can help retain good balance and body awareness, calm physical and mental stress and promote better breathing habits. They can also keep you limber and prevent injuries or imbalances caused by other activities.

These styles of movement improve your sleep in different ways. Aerobic exercise resets the sleep/wake cycle by raising body temperature then dropping it at the appropriate time before bed. As little as ten minutes of aerobic exercise can improve sleep quality and duration when performed on a regular basis. Flexibility work contributes to better posture and protects against injury, both of which will also help you sleep better. Resistance training capitalises on the growth hormone your body produces during deep sleep and uses it to form muscle, and while the research is scarce, there's evidence that the relationship goes both ways: one study found that improvements in muscle mass and function among a group of elderly adults resulted in better sleep quality.[58]

So where should you start? We'll take a look at putting together a sleep-promoting movement program in a minute. But first, I need to address the opposite issue: moving too much.

Are you moving too much?

Many Australians are too sedentary, but there are also plenty of people out there who are gym junkies. If you're reading this chapter thinking that you're all over this exercise caper and don't need to read further, this section could be for you.

Do you think you're making serious gains at the gym? Unless you're getting enough rest, think again. Neglecting your sleep seriously hampers your body's ability to build muscle. That's because growth hormone production, which facilitates muscle building and recovery, drops in step with rising sleep debt. Just twenty-four hours of sleep deprivation can slow recovery to 72% of its normal rate.

From a physiological perspective, when you leave the gym you're actually in *worse* shape than when you came in. Your stress hormones are elevated, your inflammatory biomarkers are up and even your blood sugar will be a little abnormal. Unless you give your body time to recover properly from this stressor, then it can't make the hormonal, muscular and neural adaptions it needs. And it is these adaptions that increase your fitness, improve your metabolic system, create new movement patterns and change your body composition. This is why personal trainers and exercise physiologists build what is called 'periodisation' into their training programs. They recognise that the human body requires recovery and variation in order to adapt, rather than relentless activity or constant increases in workload.

Sleep is where the true action happens. Your general energy consumption is lowered during sleep, giving your body the time it needs to grow, heal, and repair damaged tissues. It's the time your body uses to create scar tissue, the dense fibre used to repair injuries. It's the time when you generate muscle and repair the nervous system, which leads to the physical adaptions you're aiming for in your activities. Levels of human growth hormone and melatonin, both of which are critical for tissue recovery, are highest during periods of undisturbed deep sleep.

For people who are exercising a lot, it's not just a failure to prioritise sleep that can lead to poor recovery – it can actually be the exercise itself. You can become addicted to exercise, and this addiction, far from being healthy, can throw the body clock right off its course, destroy your sleep patterns and undo all your hard work in the process.

Overexercise, Jason Smith warns, sends the body into a spiral of inflammation and disrepair. The body starts working overtime to try to keep everything in good functioning order. If this state becomes chronic, the body doesn't know how to shut off, the levels of circulating hormones become too high and the adrenal glands start working double shifts.

Elite athletes understand the toll that large volumes of exercise can take on the body, and they often work with teams of experts – doctors, dieticians, massage therapists and a host of others – to ensure that they're getting the training and recovery balance just right. What's more, many of them are *paid* to professionally recover.

It's therefore more likely to be your gym junkie, aerobics addict or weekend warrior who is at risk of overtraining, burning out and ruining their sleep. So if you're doing back-to-back training sessions at your box every day, or five hours straight in the gym, stop thinking that this is healthy. This is when *eustress* (or beneficial stress) kicks over into *distress* and exercise becomes part of the problem, not the solution.

If this sounds like you, and you're in a cycle of being overtired and yet never feeling rested after a sleep, then it's time to ask yourself, 'Am I training too much?'

The right kind of fit

As you can see, getting the balance right with movement is a bit of an art. You were born to move, but not to overdo it. The quality of your sleep may well be the key to interpreting whether you've got the balance right!

You want to be the right kind of fit. And this means finding the right kind of fitness routine.

The right motivation

The main thing that gets me out of bed and into the gym at stupid o'clock is my goal to Look Good Naked. But researchers at Curtin University in Western Australia have found that people who are motivated to start exercising by guilt (just to keep your partner happy), financial commitment (because you've bought an expensive gym membership) or even the desire to achieve the beach-body ideal are unlikely to form lasting habits.[59] Instead, you're more likely to stick with a new activity if it gives you a sense of mastery and connects you with other people at the same time.[60] Looking good in the buff can be a nice side benefit, but won't keep you going long term.

If you can connect your exercise habits to something that helps other people, you'll have an even better chance of sticking with it. Acts of giving and helping others fire your 'happiness hormones': the neurochemicals dopamine, serotonin and oxytocin. We usually associate exercise just with an endorphin hit, but if you train to raise money for a charity or join with friends to support their own fitness goals, you'll be hitting the happiness trifecta, making it a whole lot easier to stick with it.[61]

The right movement

After all this talk of different types of movement, you could be feeling overwhelmed with choice.

Let's simplify things. If you're not moving much at all, then this is not the question to get stuck on. Just choose something you enjoy and get started! Richard Branson plays tennis against people who are better than him, which feeds his desire for mastery and growth and being social. Or he goes for a swim around his island, which brings him joy. So you don't have a private island, but what's your equivalent? What do you find intrinsically enjoyable? It could be walking the dog, jumping rope or joining the local lawn bowls or soccer club.

The right volume

Beware of all-or-nothing thinking, which is likely to blow up in your face. A small effort is still a great effort. Sure, you know that 150 minutes per week is the ideal minimum, but if you're nowhere near that mark yet, start with thirty, and *celebrate* when you reach that milestone. If you've just bought yourself a pedometer, don't jump straight to aiming for 10,000 steps. Start with 3,000, and give yourself a high five when you hit that goal. Be kind to yourself, pat yourself on the back and, as motivational speaker Joseph McClendon says, 'shake that ass with joy'. Your brain is wired to respond well to incremental gains.

If you're on the 'exercise junkie' end of the spectrum, then take an honest look at whether the overall volume or intensity of your weekly workload is verging on too much. Become familiar with the signs of overtraining: insomnia, depression, high resting heart rate and susceptibility to illness and injury are all red flags. If you're on the way to burnout, then cut your training volumes down, add one or two full rest days to your week and make sleep your number one priority.

The right timing

Your circadian clock suggests that the best time of day to exercise is the morning. A study conducted by Appalachian State University looked at participants who worked out at three different times – 7am, 1pm and 7pm – while monitoring their sleep quality and quantity. Participants who exercised at 7am had significantly better sleep outcomes than the other two groups.[62]

This is likely because you get your biggest spike of cortisol in the morning, and this hormone enables us to be alert and active. Exercising early reinforces this pattern of cortisol release, which in turn will ensure your body is on track for its evening slump in cortisol and the release of melatonin. Isn't your circadian rhythm clever?

That said, if you can only exercise later in the day then this is far better than not moving at all. The key is to watch your intensity. Avoid vigorous work-outs, such as heavy weights, sprint intervals or the increasingly popular HIIT (High Intensity Interval Training) routines, in the evening. These fire up the nervous system and will increase evening cortisol rather than decrease it. Instead, try more calming methods of movement in the evening.

Exercise: Your weekly work-out routine

It's time to write down your weekly routine for moving your body. Consider:

1. **Your current fitness level.** Where are you on the spectrum of sedentary to overtrained? If you're starting out, where would you start?

> 2. **Your likes and dislikes.** What kind of movement interests you? What could motivate you to try it out? What could motivate you to build it into a habit?
>
> 3. **Your balance of activities.** Do you have any physical or sporting strengths already? What areas of movement could you stand to improve? Can you incorporate different types of movement into your routine? Will you get enough rest?
>
> 4. **Your weekly schedule.** Where could movement, either formal or informal, fit into your week easily? Are you able to prioritise morning exercise?
>
> Use these questions to create a weekly movement routine for yourself.

What about pain?

When you have an acute illness or injury, you can recognise that you'll get better soon enough and can cope with short interruptions to life and sleep. But when pain becomes chronic, you experience not only the pain itself but also a load of uncertainty and worry about its cause.

Of all medical conditions, chronic pain is the most likely to cause insomnia. The pain associated with ongoing issues like arthritis, cluster headaches, back pain and fibromyalgia can make it difficult to drift off. If you're a sufferer, you probably use distraction as one of your primary pain management techniques. You read, watch TV, socialise, focus on your work or take up a hobby in order to avoid thinking about your pain. When you're getting ready for bed, however, you need to eliminate all distractions in an effort to relax and fall asleep. But when you quiet the room and dim the lights, your perception of pain can actually increase. The longer falling asleep is delayed, the more stressful the situation becomes.

You may also find yourself waking up during the night and waking earlier than desired. Research has demonstrated that individuals experiencing chronic lower back pain may experience several intense microarousals (a change in sleep state to a lighter stage of sleep) per hour of sleep, which lead to awakenings.[63] Unsurprisingly, you're therefore likely to start the new day feeling like rubbish as well.

In an extremely unfair catch-22, sleep deprivation also makes people who suffer from chronic conditions less resistant to pain, because the lack of sleep keeps your sympathetic nervous system on high alert.

For many people, the answer is to take pain medication. When you're desperate to shut off the pain and get to sleep, reaching for the painkillers is understandable, but it's not a sustainable solution. Opioids don't address the root cause of your pain; they simply mask the pain sensation. While this may offer short-term relief, long-term use of opioids brings risk of hormonal damage as well as addiction. Here's a disturbing statistic: in Australia currently, two-thirds more people die from complications arising from opioid addiction, or from accidental prescription medication overdose, than from heroin.[64]

Thankfully, pain science has come along in leaps and bounds in recent decades, and pain scientists have discovered safer ways to reverse patterns of chronic pain. Pain is more complex than we used to believe, but it is also far more treatable … if you're willing to engage in new styles of treatment. The two key ways to tackle it are through re-education and movement. Here's how.

Get a pain re-education

Pain is a protector. In older models of pain science, pain was thought to indicate damage at the site of the tissue (whether bone, muscle, ligament or nerve). In newer models, it is understood that pain is always produced in the brain, not at the site of the tissue, and the level of pain depends on your brain's interpretation of the circumstances and how much danger you're in. This is true in 100% of cases. We've all read stories of people losing their limbs and only feeling a mild bump – and equally intriguing stories of people who have lost a limb experiencing excruciating phantom pain![65] The pain you feel is real, but it is not a reliable indicator of whether a part of your body is damaged or in danger.

Fear about the meaning of your pain worsens pain and keeps it going. So after getting checked out for the rare nasties that could really do you harm – cancers and the like – the first step to recovery is learning that pain, though real and debilitating, does not always indicate damage. And damaged tissue does not always lead to pain! Many people with bulging and protruding intervertebral discs experience no pain whatsoever.[66]

Simply removing fear from the equation can speed up the healing process immensely. The research backs this up. Back pain sufferers who learnt about recent findings in pain biology showed a decrease in disability and pain sensation during previously painful tasks.[67]

And fibromyalgia sufferers who learnt that emotional and mental stressors can perpetuate physical symptoms greatly diminish their symptoms.[68]

Pain re-education works. To get the ball rolling, ask yourself the following questions about your pain sensations and beliefs:

> *What do I think this pain means? What do I think is causing it? What is my biggest fear about it?*
>
> *Are there times my pain is noticeably worse or better? Do I notice any patterns in my pain response?*
>
> *What stressors in my life could be contributing to an overly excitable pain response?*

Get moving – slowly

If you have ongoing pain, you may also have stopped moving much for fear of making things worse. This makes total sense. After all, the pain response is trying to protect you and stopping you from performing movements your brain considers threatening. But once you have accepted the idea that pain doesn't equal damage, you can start to move again.

Gradual re-exposure to activity teaches your brain that movement is safe and not harmful, reducing the 'threat perception' that is causing the protective response of pain in the first place. This could take time, but it's far more productive than simply drugging yourself for the pain every day. The best way forward is to find an activity that you enjoy and build towards that – so go back to the previous section, *The right kind of fit*, and figure out what will work for you.

If you're nervous about re-engaging in activity, find a good health professional who will partner with you to set some goals and work towards them. Jason Smith suggests taking an 'early interventionist' approach to pain, taking any niggles, feelings of fatigue or hints of pain straight for a check-in with your trusted health coach. I'll go into how to find a great health professional in chapter 10, *Your Dream Team*.

Get comfortable in bed

Finally, for those with recurring pain conditions who are struggling to sleep, it's helpful to make sure that your sleep set-up is comfortable and your sleep posture is not itself contributing to pain amplification.

According to the US-based Better Sleep Council, the most beneficial sleeping position is on the side, with the legs slightly raised and towards the chest. This position is ideal because it allows you to maintain curvature of the spine, which promotes a more comfortable and restful night's sleep. Side sleeping also keeps your airways clear and eases digestive problems like heartburn.

If you're a tummy sleeper, here are my top strategies to get you out of the habit:

- Buy an echidna and place it next to your belly. When you roll onto your stomach, you will be stabbed in a thousand places, which will encourage you back onto your side.
- Ask your romantic partner to stay awake all night, rolling you onto your side whenever they notice you on your belly. This should work well for your sleep posture, but you can say goodbye to your sex life.

- If neither of those work, buy a couple of spare pillows. Hug one to your chest and prop one between your knees to stop you from rolling onto your belly. If your partner feels left out, loan them the echidna.

Jokes aside, getting comfortable in bed will require a supportive mattress, but one that also provides enough fluidity so that your shoulders and hips can sink in slightly. You can learn more about finding a good mattress fit in chapter 8. Pain re-education and getting yourself moving again will nudge your pain-insomnia cycle in a more positive direction, and a comfy sleep set-up will be the cherry on top.

Speaking of cherries, it's time to delve into the sleep-nutrition connection.

6. EATING WELL: THE INGREDIENTS FOR A GOOD NIGHT'S SLEEP

Confession time: I'm always getting sucked in by nutrition click bait. Show me a headline like 'Is Eating Egg Yolks as Bad as Smoking?' and I'm like a moth to a flame. The only problem is, I don't know how to sort out the hype from the truth.

We get bombarded daily with new ideas about how we should be eating for optimal health. Should we be eating like our Palaeolithic ancestors, subsisting on meat and avoiding grains? Or should we be vegan, avoiding all animal products? Yesterday fat was bad for us and today it's good for us – or maybe just some forms of it? Are we all addicted to sugar? Are carbohydrates evil?

It's easy to feel like a deer stuck in the headlights in the complex world of modern nutrition. Our culture has two extremes: either not caring what we eat and when, and overdoing it, or obsessing over weight loss fads, extreme diets, and looking a certain way. Some of us sit at one end, some at the other. Most of us – and I'm as guilty as anyone – flip-flop wildly between the two extremes, starting a new cleanse or eating regimen each Monday morning but going back to our usual habits in time for Friday evening.

The impulse to eat well is a good one. I believe that food is medicine, and putting the good stuff into your body is a big part of learning the art of self-leadership. It's also an area I've not been brilliant at for various reasons, some of which I'll share over the coming pages, so I've drawn on the wisdom of people who really get these things to explain what 'eating well' actually means, and how it relates to sleeping well.

If there's one thing I *do* know, it's this: the better you eat, the better you'll sleep, and the better you sleep, the better you'll eat. So I'll start with what 'eating well' really means, then address the big one: how to lose weight without losing sleep.

Why quality is key

Let's look at the big-picture stuff first: diet quality.

You've probably noticed that lots of the talk about food and diet quality these days centres around 'gut health' – and for good reason. The gut, or enteric nervous system, has a bidirectional relationship with the central nervous system. This is sometimes referred to as the 'gut-brain axis'. Recent research is turning up all kinds of interesting links between the health of your gut flora (the bacteria that live in your GI tract) and your mental and metabolic health – so much so that the scientific community has taken to calling the lining of the gut the 'second brain'.[69]

Because your gastrointestinal tract is lined with lots of nerve cells, it guides your emotions as well as your digestion. Your gut is not simply your body's waste management unit, breaking down and reusing what material it can before sending the waste product down the disposal unit. It also responds to what you put into it, which has a huge impact on how you think and feel. Think about this: 95% of your serotonin, the neurotransmitter that helps regulate sleep and appetite, mediate your moods and inhibit pain, is found in your gut.[70] And your serotonin function is highly influenced by the quality of your gut bacteria – which in turn is influenced by what you stick in your mouth in the first place.

At this point, as a non-expert in the field of nutrition, I start feeling a little overwhelmed by all the big concepts and words like 'microbiome' and 'neurotransmitter'. The take home is this: what you put in your mouth affects your mood and your sleep.

It might help to think of your gut as less like an inanimate garbage disposal unit and more like a person. A sensitive person. A guy called Gary Gut. Gary's like that middle manager in your office whose mood affects the whole vibe of your workplace. When Gary is happy, everyone's happy. The workplace hums with productivity and energy and fun. When Gary's not so happy, everyone creeps off to their own cubicle and tries to stay out of his way. Communication slows down, productivity slows down and things begin to fall apart.

So what kind of diet keeps Gary Gut happy and healthy? According to founder of the Wellness Guys, nutritionist and chiropractor Damien Kristof, it's all about food quality. 'Forget about counting calories, food points or tracking things with an app,' says Damien. 'Instead of worrying about whether you should be eating high or low fat, high or low protein, high or low carbohydrate, start thinking instead: am I eating *good* fats, carbohydrates and proteins?'

It's easy to get hung up on how much you're eating rather than food quality. Damien suggests taking the focus off any type of counting or measuring for a while and stocking your kitchen with nutrient-dense whole foods such as healthy fats, plenty of fresh vegetables, quality meats and fish and grains – whether gluten containing, or gluten free if you need it. A diet rich in whole, real foods will regulate your appetite and encourage you to tune in to your true hunger levels.

These sources of quality nutrients line up with traditional diets, like the Mediterranean diet and the traditional Japanese diet. Studies comparing traditional and Western diet patterns have shown that the risk of depression is 25%–35% lower for those sticking to traditional, less processed patterns of eating.[71] The foundation for the Mediterranean way of eating, for example, is lots of vegetables, nuts, seeds, legumes and pulses (like white beans and lentils), whole grains (like barley and millet), herbs, spices, fish, seafood and extra virgin olive oil. On top of that there's a moderate consumption of poultry, eggs and dairy foods, and the rare consumption of red meat.

Traditional diets are far lower in processed and refined foods and sugars (think most pre-packaged foods like crackers and biscuits, white bread and many cereals), which can trigger inflammation and the release of stress hormones. These older diets also contain fermented foods – things like yoghurt, sauerkraut and Kim chi – which act as natural probiotics and increase the 'good' bacteria in the gut. What's more, where such diets rely on traditional farming methods, they avoid the use of pesticides like glyphosate, used in industrial farming. The World Health Organization has declared this chemical 'unlikely to pose carcinogenic risk' for humans at current exposure levels, but this is hardly a ringing endorsement for its use. It's just another chemical stressor with as yet unclear consequences for modern humans.[72]

A higher-quality diet will improve your sleep quality. A US study of over 5,500 people found that 'normal sleepers' (those sleeping between seven and nine hours a night) ate the greatest food variety and had an increased consumption of complex carbohydrates (whole grain foods) and vitamins and minerals.[73] If you focus on good-quality foods from natural sources, you'll get all the vitamins and minerals you need for all-round health. These include B vitamins, magnesium, zinc and calcium, all of which play a role in producing good-quality sleep.

I've noticed this personally in my recent shift to more organic produce. I can be a bit tight-fisted when it comes to grocery spending, so I've never wanted to pay more for organic stuff. But my fiancée, Juliana, has insisted that we need to buy the highest quality foods we can. I've been sourcing organic produce and eating more fruits and vegetables overall – and it feels fantastic.

Exercise: Improve your diet

What does a normal week of eating look like for you? If you don't know what you eat and when, observe your patterns this week and write them down.

> Once you've taken a look, write down some ways you could improve the quality of your diet and keep your gut happy.
>
> Where can you fit in more fruits and vegetables?
>
> How can you improve the quality of your fats, proteins and carbohydrates?
>
> Is it possible to opt for organic sources?

Minimising sleep saboteurs

Getting good sleep starts with good nutrient intake, but it doesn't end there. Deriving nutrients from your food sources is not just a matter of putting the right things into your body, but being aware of things that can hamper your body's absorption and use of these nutrients.

Here's some news that probably won't surprise you: coffee, soft drinks, alcohol and pharmaceutical drugs are all nutrient depletors. I've taken to calling these the nutritional party poopers. Much as I love a cup of coffee (or six), I'm now aware that drinking the stuff leaches the calcium, magnesium, potassium and sodium out of my body more quickly. Alcohol also speeds up losses of these nutrients, along with damaging zinc and iron stores. And all of these nutrients are needed for serotonin and melatonin production. Knowing this now doesn't mean I've gone for total abstinence, but it certainly gives me more motivation to watch what goes into my system.

For the sake of your sleep, it's important to watch your coffee and alcohol intake anyway. These guys are notorious sleep saboteurs. Consuming caffeine less than six hours before going to bed can negatively affect your rest. That's because caffeine stays in your body for a long time, and can fragment your sleep cycles long after the caffeine high wears off. And despite popular belief, alcohol will not help you sleep better. A single glass of wine may help you relax, but the later stages of alcohol metabolism interfere with deeper phases of your sleep cycles, so you will likely wake up feeling tired despite having spent enough time in bed. All the more reason why I should emulate Richard Branson in my drinking habits!

Medications frequently interfere with absorption too, by binding with vitamins and minerals before they're absorbed in the bloodstream and taking them out as waste product. This is not just 'big meds' like tranquilisers, sedatives, opiates and antibiotics. Even just popping an antacid interferes with the workings of the GI tract and prevents absorption of much-needed vitamins and minerals.[74] Sometimes the benefits and necessities of taking medications far outweigh the risk, so it's not necessary to avoid them altogether, but it certainly gives pause for thought when you realise the cost of regular consumption.

> **Exercise: Take control of your sleep saboteurs**
>
> Which nutritional party poopers turn up regularly in your life? What are your patterns of caffeine, alcohol and medication consumption? Could these be having a negative impact on your sleep? How could you moderate your intake?

Lose weight, not sleep

We've looked at how what you eat influences your sleep. But now it starts to get tricky. Because guess what? How you sleep also influences what you eat!

Turning down an extra piece of cake is much harder on insufficient sleep. Hunger is regulated by two hormones called leptin and ghrelin. Simply put: less leptin equals more hunger, and more ghrelin equals more hunger. Sleep deprivation suppresses leptin and stimulates ghrelin, making you that much hungrier, even if you've eaten enough. Sleep deprivation also impairs the part of your brain that controls complex decision-making, leaving you without the discipline you need to stick to a healthy eating plan.

And if you thought that was the end of it, being sleep deprived also spikes your levels of cortisol. An overabundance of cortisol leads to increased fat storage around the abdomen, among other problems. Not sleeping enough also drops your body's sensitivity to insulin, which increases fat storage as well – this time in dangerous places like your liver. So if you're a frequent short sleeper, you are more likely to have a lowered metabolism and wider waist circumference than your long-sleeping counterpart, even if you manage to knuckle down and avoid the junk food![75]

If you're someone who needs to lose a bit of weight, I know what you're thinking right now. 'Let me get this straight: to lose weight I need to consume less energy, but this disturbs sleep, which causes increased appetite, which leads to weight gain! What kind of special hell is this?'

It's the ultimate Catch-22.

Believe me, I've been there. At a few points in my life, I've found myself overweight – and I'm not talking about a few 'vanity' kilos. As a child, I was obese. Mum was overweight as well. We weren't well off and she always wanted to save money, so she'd buy out-of-date food for us, stuff that was cheap and nutritionally bad. I didn't know anything about nutrition at that point. I was probably 110kg by the age of fourteen, and my weight stayed up there until I was seventeen and 180cm. My parents had split up when I was three, and when I look back now I can see that I used to eat to feel good – to feel loved and whole.

At the age of seventeen, I started to notice women and realised that I wanted to look good for them. I decided to lose weight, and I actually lost 23kg in eight weeks. I did that through rather extreme dieting: a massive breakfast, a massive lunch, and celery and carrots for dinner. And I exercised hard every single day.

This was effective for a time. Then at age twenty-four I found some success when I was in advertising. I started to earn a lot of money. I lost my way with my core values, and put on massive weight again. I was overweight for about three or four years, and I was in a relationship where that was acceptable so I decided weight loss wasn't a major priority to me. Then that relationship broke up and suddenly I realised I needed to get healthy again!

I know what it's like to be overweight and to be stuck in a yo-yoing weight loss pattern. These days I'm down to a healthy weight again and have maintained it for a long time. What I've learnt during my time working with lots of great people in the sleep and wellness industries is this comes from a focus on health, not weight.

Lots of people want to rip the Band-Aid off with weight loss, like I did the first time around. They go hard: they exercise heavily and restrict food intake and try to get it all over and done with. I'm not going to tell you it will never work, because it did work for me – for a time. There's some evidence that rapid initial weight loss can be effective.[76] But the thing that really makes weight loss stick, whether you do it fast or slow, is a bunch of small, healthy habit changes that you can keep for life.

If you don't intend to drink replacement shakes for the rest of your life, don't use replacement shakes to lose weight. If you don't want to have cabbage soup three meals a day for the rest of your life, don't do the cabbage soup diet. Start as you mean to continue – by building a healthy lifestyle with low work stress, good amounts of movement, a quality diet based on whole foods and a whole lot of sleep.

Here are my tips for taking care of your weight and sleep at the same time.

Minimise your energy gap

Have you ever gone on a diet only to find yourself unable to fall asleep, or waking up in the early hours with a growling stomach? That's because your brain is trying to protect you from starvation. When your body is threatened with energy restriction (which, as far as it knows, could be permanent) it sends distress messages to the brain, which responds by pumping out stress hormones like adrenaline and cortisol. This is yet another example of the fight or flight response.

If your under-eating is severe or goes on for a long time, you will experience one of two responses. The first is rebound eating. After days of ignoring the morning tea tray at work and holding back at social events, you'll suddenly find yourself gobbling everything in sight. This is not because you're a pathetic person who has no willpower; it's because your brain cares about you and wants you to live. The desire to eat everything RIGHT NOW is a protective response, designed by your brain to restore energy equilibrium. This is why yo-yo dieting is such a common problem.

The second response is downward adaption. If you've pushed through a rebound period and not given up on your under-eating, your body will slow down all its processes in order to conserve energy. Signs of this adaption can include:

- Sleep disturbance
- Digestive issues like gas, bloating, constipation or diarrhoea
- Reflux or heartburn
- Low energy and fatigue
- Reduced libido
- Fluid retention
- Anxiety and depression
- Loss of muscle mass
- Low immunity and recurring illnesses

Sounds fun, doesn't it? It just goes to show that your body operates best when it knows it has a ready supply of food.

Therefore, it's important to keep your energy reduction moderate and sustainable. This is the best way to stop your body or mind feeling too deprived, it's the best way to encourage long-term adherence to your new habits, and it's also the best way to keep your sleep quality up. So instead of cutting out full meals or food groups (like carbs), it's a good idea to simply lower portion sizes by a little bit across the whole day.

Have you noticed how dinner plates are now so big they need their own postcode? They might look glamorous, but for those of us who like to finish everything on the plate (or are conditioned to do so) they're a portion-control disaster. I've found that I can reduce my food intake almost without noticing by replacing big dinner plates with smaller side plates. This could work wonders for you, too. A small shift in habits like this can be incorporated with little social or psychological cost and your sleep will probably not be affected at all!

Work to keep your muscle mass

If you're going to lose some of your body weight, make sure it comes from fat, not muscle.

How can you retain muscle? First, prioritise some form of regular resistance training several times a week. When a ship is sinking, the crew throw jetsam (anything deemed not immediately useful) overboard into the water in order to lighten the load. When your body is losing weight, it chucks out the least useful material first. If you're inactive, it will see your muscle as less useful than your fat, which at least is a source of stored energy. Convince your body that your muscle tissue is in use, and it will stay on board! Whether you use light weights, heavy weights, your own body weight or resistance bands doesn't really matter – just get that muscle moving.

Second, eat a form of protein at every meal. This could be eggs, yoghurt, nuts, meat, fish or tofu. Keeping your protein intake high helps your muscles repair and retain mass. As a bonus, a high-protein breakfast will also help your body produce dopamine, which will make you feel more awake in the morning and keep your circadian clock on track.

Time your carbs and fats for better sleep

Timing of carbs and fats doesn't matter from a weight loss point of view, just from a 'what's going to keep you awake or help you sleep' point of view. Eating regular meals that contain all the main groups – carbs, fats and proteins – is the best way to keep your metabolism happy, but if you tip the balance of carbohydrates up a bit later in the day, this could help to slow your body down and prepare for sleep. Although many people like to advise eating light at night for weight loss, you're making your life a lot harder if you're avoiding food (and particularly carbs) at night. When I was eating just celery and carrots at night, I had great difficulty getting to sleep.

As you head towards bedtime, you're looking for slow-release energy to help you wind down. A slow-digesting carbohydrate will allow serotonin to level up with dopamine in the brain, while the addition of fat can assist in regulating blood sugar levels throughout the night.

This could mean an evening meal that includes some sweet potato with butter, or a pre-bed snack of a handful of nuts. I'm a big fan of macadamias and almonds.

Sort out your stress first

Recognise that weight loss is stressful for your body, so minimise other life stressors before you try to do anything funky with your energy intake. If you're an accountant, don't embark on your weight loss mission during tax return season. If you've started a new job or a new relationship, don't throw another change on the pile. Wait until life is relatively stable and then start making changes. This will allow your body to focus on just one stressful task at a time.

Something else that will keep stress at bay is to schedule regular 'diet breaks' into your diet. This means taking a day or two every few weeks where you deliberately eat more. It may seem counterintuitive, but this practice actually encourages weight loss! As we've seen, scarcity can send your body into down-regulation if it goes on for too long. But if you allow a day or two of abundance, your brain will be reassured by the presence of extra energy and will keep your metabolism firing happily. Eating a bit more for a few days also gives you a mental break from the effort of being more careful with your food intake.

Finally, treat yourself and your eating habits with kindness. Damien Kristof, while being a huge advocate of eating well, says he can't underscore this point enough. For food to enhance our lives, it needs to be a nurturer, not a source of stress. Faddish eating, Damien says, can cause social isolation. 'I often say, you're far better eating a slice of bread with your mates than sitting in the corner sucking on a kale smoothie by yourself.' When we bounce between restrictive food fads and unhealthy patterns of food as comfort and reward, it's confusing to our bodies.

The healthiest populations with the greatest longevity and life quality are the least stressed ones. Successfully aging populations don't bio-hack or swing from one 'optimal diet' to the next; they just enjoy fresh food, eat seasonally and take their time with it all. On a recent trip around the Greek Islands, I was struck by the lack of overweight people. These guys drank wine almost daily and ate homemade bread, pasta dishes and desserts along with their fresh fish and produce. They enjoyed their meals and lingered over them. They seemed to be really in tune with their appetites and regulated themselves easily. Maybe this has something to do with the Mediterranean diet suiting Mediterranean people best – I'll leave that to the nutrition experts to figure out. But whatever foods we choose to eat, we can learn a lot from their approach to enjoyment and moderation.

Quality nutrition, enjoyment, moderation and good sleep – that sounds like a great recipe for healthy, happy living to me.

7. LOVING WELL: THE ART OF SLEEPING TOGETHER

A bad night's sleep almost ruined my love life.

My fiancée, Juliana, and I were travelling in Greece. We'd just become engaged in Athens and were having the most romantic trip of our lives. Everything was glorious: we'd quad-biked around the islands, from Mykonos, sampling some of the finest food you could ever taste, through to Santorini, where we drifted around on a yacht, with a saxophonist playing the music of love while we watched the sun dive beneath the ocean. It couldn't have been more of a dream come true.

Then we arrived in Crete. Our first mistake was arriving late at night. Feeling tired and drained, we hired a car and started driving. And we drove for two hours. In Crete, no one drives slowly – there are no speed cameras so everyone's going at about 180km/h – so we were driving in pitch black, concentrating hard to stay on the right side of the road. Finally, we reached our destination – a romantic hotel in the old town of Chania. I had spent so much time for this trip organising the most romantic hotels that I could find. This one had a balcony overlooking the bay – it was going to be fabulous.

We arrived at 11pm, checked in and jumped into bed. Then, things started going downhill. We were lying on the worst mattress I've ever encountered: an old-school Bonnell spring mattress – a very basic spring system with nothing but a layer of sheet over the springs. Ever the optimist, I thought to myself, 'We can handle this. We can just get through it. We'll just sleep tonight and we'll get through it.'

But then I noticed something else. Our room was over the biggest nightclub in all of Crete. I'm not talking lovely, sensual Greek folk music; I'm talking *doof doof*, *thump thump*, right outside our room. By 1am, Juliana and I were both going insane. My darling Colombian fiancée gave me some earplugs from the plane, but they did absolutely nothing. At 2am I called the manager and screamed down the phone, 'I paid good money for this hotel room. This is unacceptable. This needs to be fixed.' He promised to sort us out in the morning.

But after another hour of this torture, my whole mind was going. I became a determined, angry monster. I started getting angry at Juliana, as though she was a she-devil. I charged downstairs, back to the phone (this was an old-school hotel with one phone in the lobby). I said, 'Listen here. You get down here right now and you sort this out. I'm not sleeping. I'm not going to have my holiday ruined by you and this hotel. You fix this now.' What I felt like yelling was, 'If you don't fix this, okay, I'm going to set fire to the entire building.'

By 4am, the manager had arrived. He took us to another of his hotels down the road, where we fell into an exhausted stupor for the next day.

I'm the first person to admit that I'm a lousy partner when I'm sleep deprived. When I'm well-rested, the loving energy flows freely for me, and I find it easy to connect to my fiancée. But when I've had a few nights of poor sleep, suddenly I lose all sense of reality and I start thinking she's growing horns. For me, good sleep is the key to connecting well and relating in a loving way.

While many of us think of sleep as an individual thing, you don't sleep in a vacuum. Most people will, at some point in life, share a bed with another person. The quality of your sleep will have an impact on the quality – and perhaps the longevity – of that relationship! And, for better or for worse, that relationship will have an impact on the quantity and quality of your sleep.

If you're not motivated enough already by all the benefits of getting better sleep, then think about this: being sleep deprived can thwart your success in romantic relationships. Now, this seems obvious. When you're tired, you're irritable, less able to connect well emotionally and usually a bit off in the libido department, too.

It's not just your ability to connect that takes a nosedive when you're sleep deprived, however. Bad sleep also makes you less attractive to other people. Swedish scientists conducted a study where participants were subjected to two days of sleep deprivation before having their photographs rated for attractiveness, health, trustworthiness and social appeal.[77] Sleep-deprived participants were perceived as less attractive and less healthy, and the researchers concluded that 'sleep affects facial appearance negatively and decreases others' willingness to socialise with the sleep-restricted person.' It seems that beauty sleep is real, after all.

Similar sleep-and-relationship studies have found that sleep deprivation causes people to lack a sense of humour, feel more insecure, jump too quickly into conflict and struggle with decision-making – all of which tend to kill the romance. Whether you're looking to meet someone or have an established relationship, taking care of yourself by fostering healthy sleeping habits is going to heighten your chances of making things work.

But what about the other side of the coin – the impact of your relationship on sleep? If you have a significant other, then the quality of that relationship can influence your sleep. As one piece of research summarises: 'In a high-functioning relationship, a partner is likely to be a powerful stress-buffer, down-regulating physiological and psychological stress responses, promoting salutary health behaviours, and deterring against health behaviours that could have a negative impact on sleep. In contrast, distressed relationships are a primary source of stress, leading to heightened physiological and emotional arousal, poor health behaviours, and ultimately greater risk for sleep disturbance and sleep disorders.'[78]

In this chapter we'll tackle three of the biggest issues that can impact sleep for couples: snoring, scheduling issues and relational drift.

Snoring

Imagine (or recall, depending on your situation) being in the middle of a pleasant dream, only to be jarred awake by the throaty rumble of your partner's snoring. This is the reality for countless couples across Australia. Alongside the strain it can place on relationships, snoring can be a signal of underlying health problems. But since many people think it's a benign condition, they're unlikely to see their doctor about it. Here's what causes snoring and when you should seek medical intervention.

When you sleep, your throat narrows and your tongue falls backwards. The walls of your throat vibrate as you breathe in and out, and for certain people – mostly men, though snoring affects every population group to some degree – the vibrations are loud enough to wake up a sleeping partner. The narrower the opening in your upper airway, the louder the vibration.

Some people are just anatomically predisposed to snore. They may have larger tongues, thicker necks, an overbite, jaw tension or weaker nerves controlling the tongue. Snorers could also have an anatomical abnormality, like enlarged adenoids or tonsils or a deviated septum. Allergies or an illness leading to respiratory inflammation could also narrow the airway and lead to snoring. Muscle relaxants taken before bed, including alcohol, can also be a factor. Being overweight can add to the troubles as extra tissues and poor tone in and around the neck and throat contribute to pressure on the airway.

Perhaps the most insidious cause is a condition known as obstructive sleep apnea. This condition occurs when an airway collapses or becomes blocked while you sleep, leading to breathing pauses and loud snoring. A person with sleep apnea will typically be forced out of deep sleep into light sleep to gasp for breath throughout the night. About one in three men and one in five women who snore regularly also have sleep apnea.

Sleep apnea, when left untreated, is dangerous. Breathing pauses interrupt your sleep, leaving you chronically deprived of deep sleep and its important restorative benefits. Sleep apnea is also dangerous for your heart, increasing your risk of irregular heartbeat, heart attacks, heart failure, stroke and other serious conditions.

The relational cost of leaving obstructive sleep apnea untreated is now also receiving more attention in sleep research, and it's not great news. Chronic snoring not only causes relationship friction because it sounds unsexy and interrupts sleep, but it also tanks your libido. Studies show a clear correlation between obstructive sleep apnea and sexual difficulties, both subjective (feeling a lack of connection or desire for intimacy with a partner) and objective (problems with arousal and orgasm for both men and women, and erectile dysfunction for men).[79]

If you or your partner are snoring, it's likely that neither of you are getting the sleep you need, so it's time to go in search of solutions.

Before we do that, however, let's address the elephant in the room. Which one of you is the snorer? Is it you or is it your partner? (No, you can't blame it on the elephant!)

If it's you, that's actually good news! You're already reading this book and you are therefore ready to step up and become the master of your own health. You are motivated to address your sleep problems and you have many of the tools already at your disposal. I have addressed the following section to you as though *you* are the snorer. And if you are, all you need to do is follow through on the ideas below to start getting some relief.

If it's your partner, things may be trickier. As life coach Ben Carvosso says, you can't change other people. You can have desires for other people, but not goals. Therefore, you can only take responsibility for your own part in the relationship. Yes, you can wave this book under your partner's nose, or leave it subtly on their pillow, but unless they're ready and motivated to address things for themselves, dropping hints or nagging won't produce change. However, this doesn't leave you powerless. In fact, recognising that you are not responsible for your partner's behaviour will free you from that burden and allow you to focus on your own needs. If you're the snorer, get to it and take some action! If you're not, I have a word of advice for you at the end.

So, to the snoring solutions.

1. Cull the obvious culprits

Anti-snore mouth guards, chin straps, nose plugs, tongue stabilisers ... Google the phrase 'stop me snoring' and you'll discover all sorts of innovative (and possibly crazy) suggestions out there to eliminate your noisy little issue. Many of these may be worth a try, but it's sensible (and less costly) to start with the obvious things. Are you drinking too much alcohol, particularly at night? Cut it out for a few weeks and see what happens. What about smoking or other drugs that may be acting as a relaxant? All of these should be investigated before you start buying anti-snoring devices. Now is the time to consider what they're doing to your sleep anyway, and revisit whether you want these things in your life.

Or there could be a respiratory issue or allergy that you need to get under control. Alongside things like dust mite and pet hair allergies or seasonal allergic reactions, eating particular foods could be triggering respiratory distress. For some people, certain foods can cause some inflammatory reaction in the sinuses, blocking up the airways. One friend of mine (let's call him Jack Hammer) was frustrated by what appeared to be random bouts of loud snoring. Then he noticed a pattern: he only snored on the nights when his girlfriend brought over a block of his favourite dark chocolate. Now Jack is careful to consume it in smaller amounts and earlier in the day, if at all, and his snoring no longer wakes the neighbourhood.

2. Fix your posture

Snoring that comes and goes can often be alleviated by a change of sleeping posture. We all have different mouth and throat anatomy, and some of us just can't sleep on our backs without blocking off the airways.

But how can you change posture when you're unconscious? Apart from asking your partner to kick you, there are a few solutions. There's the old 'sew a tennis ball into the back of your pyjamas' trick, which works by causing pain when you try to lie on your back and sending you back to a side-lying or front position. You could try one of the variety of mouth, tongue or chin splints on the market instead, in the hope that these will keep your airways clear whatever sleeping position you end up in.

A less uncomfortable and potentially more permanent option is to try hypnosis. You might wonder how a few autosuggestions can help with what appear to be anatomical obstructive issues. Well, according to one website, the unconscious mind controls all of our muscles and postural alignment at night, just as it does during the day. Therefore, hypnosis can 'teach your unconscious mind to help keep the right amount of muscle tone and monitor your airways as you sleep, and keep the airways open to allow you to breathe easily and quietly throughout the night.'[80]

London hypnosis practitioner David Kraft shares a great case study of Lilly, a slim and healthy twenty-five-year-old woman who came to him for treatment after twelve years of snoring and many failed medical interventions including sleep studies, a nasal endoscopy, and the use of numerous decongestants and inhalers. David taught Lilly the art of self-hypnosis over two sessions, during which they worked on embedding new postural habits and relearning the art of sleeping like a child. After just two sessions, Lilly's twelve-year snoring problem and the social isolation that came with it were gone. She could now unconsciously correct her own sleep posture and breathe in the relaxed, easy manner of her own childhood sleep.[81]

3. Try CPAP

If snoring doesn't respond to habit or posture changes, you may have obstructive sleep apnea and it's time to be examined by a doctor. Your healthcare professional will consider your age, lifestyle habits and other factors and come up with a suitable treatment plan. The approaches they are likely to recommend are the two tried and true treatments for sleep apnea: weight loss, and the use of continuous positive airway pressure (known as CPAP).

The link between excess weight and sleep apnea is well established, and for this reason it's the first approach that doctors recommend. However, when some doctors set a weight loss target for their patients, they see it as a means to an end and don't consider the mode of weight loss, sometimes even advocating for drastic approaches like gastric band surgery in order to reach weight targets quickly. But as we've seen, when you're struggling with both excess weight and poor sleep, you're caught between a rock and a hard place! Your poor sleep is causing your body to hold onto weight, and pushing weight loss too fast may backfire by interfering further with sleep and driving down the metabolism.

If weight loss is recommended for you, take the long-term approach with small, sustainable habit changes as we discussed in the last chapter. In the meantime, CPAP could actually assist your weight loss efforts. Getting enough oxygen overnight and improving your sleep could be *the* key for recovering your metabolic health and making the better lifestyle choices that will see those excess kilos start to melt away. You'll definitely have a better chance of implementing your new habits when you're not existing in an oxygen-starved state.

Many people struggle to comply with CPAP treatment. Let's face it, wearing a mask over your nose and mouth and being attached to a noisy oxygen pump all night is uncomfortable, inconvenient and downright unsexy. But persistence with CPAP will pay off, eventually reversing all the side effects of sleep deprivation for you, including any of those pesky sexual dysfunctions and mood issues you might have experienced.[82]

4. Partners, fit your own mask first!

Now, a word to long-suffering partners of snorers.

If you're the partner of a snorer, I suggest approaching this issue with a 'Fit Your Own Oxygen Mask First' philosophy. And no, I don't mean getting a twin CPAP machine so you can breathe like Darth Vader alongside your loved one. I mean this: take care of your own sleep needs so that you can support your partner.

You know the drill. You're on an aeroplane and the flight attendant goes through the safety instructions. When it comes to an emergency, you're told, you must get your own oxygen supply sorted out before helping others. Being the well-mannered, altruistic person that you are, you wonder about this etiquette. Shouldn't the able-bodied be dashing about fitting masks on all the small children, the elderly and the infirm? Then it dawns on you – if you're unable to breathe, you'll be unconscious fairly quickly, and an unconscious person is very little help to others. You make a mental note of where your mask sits, and remind yourself that it's quite okay to put yours on first.

Take this self-care philosophy into the rest of your life and you'll find that, rather than making you selfish, it will make you a better person and far more useful to others. If your beloved is taking a proactive approach to their snoring, fantastic! Do what you can to support and encourage them. If you can, stick with them in the same bed. Studies have shown that sleep apnea patients who use CPAP therapy are 60% more likely to stick with the treatment if their partners continue to share a bed, rather than sleeping separately.[83] However, don't feel bad about protecting your own sleep needs. If this means buying earplugs or moving into your own room, just do it. Be open about your own needs without assigning blame, and ask your partner how you can show them love and support outside snoring hours. Your relationship may even be stronger for it.

Incompatible body clocks

If you and your partner have average circadian rhythms (which, as you'll recall, almost 70% of us do), you likely have similar sleep patterns. But put a night owl and a lark together, and you'll have some difficulty marrying their sleep schedules. What do you do if your body clocks are out of sync?

This very real issue can cause tension due to a clash of expectations. This is due in part to the unspoken expectation in modern relationships that couples must share a bedroom, and preferably a sleep schedule, in order to demonstrate proper investment and healthy emotional attachment. Yet bed-sharing norms have varied wildly across times and cultures, ranging from the all-in-together style of household co-sleeping in pre-industrial times to the more uptight 'separate rooms for all' model in Victorian England. Within the field of sleep psychology, studies on 'sleep concordance' (shared sleep schedules and matched sleep cycles) show that there's some link between coordinated schedules and relationship satisfaction, but the correlation is not clear and it seems to differ between men and women.[84] So, while many people report that they sleep better with a partner, and many therapists continue to sing the praises of co-sleeping or coordinating sleep schedules for couples, it's an area that can be approached with creativity.

Sleep incompatibility is a far more common issue than many people realise. It's not something I've personally experienced, but my friends Carl and Louise have opened my eyes to the world of circadian-rhythm-challenged romance. These lovebirds discovered they weren't 'birds of a feather' early on. Louise had always been an early riser, although when she met Carl she was still in recovery mode from a year of night shifts and was working her way back to normalcy. Meanwhile, Carl was a die-hard night owl. When the two started sleeping over at each other's houses, Louise would get tired and head for bed around 9pm, while Carl would stay up for a few more hours. As soon as he joined her, however, Louise would be tossing and turning, unable to get back to sleep. Then she would be up at 5:30am, tip-toeing around the place while Carl was still sleeping in his room. Carl also became anxious about disturbing Louise, and found that his sleep quality dropped considerably. They could see it was going to be a problem.

What are the options if you're in a situation like Carl and Louise? We'll come back to them in a minute, but first let's look at some possibilities: co-exist as you are in the same room, try to align schedules or opt for separate rooms.

Co-existing on different sleep schedules can work if you're both resilient sleepers, not easily disturbed by your partner fumbling around or turning on the light. This approach will require communication and consideration about helpful space-sharing tactics. Will the night owl stay out of the bedroom for late-night reading, or is the bedside lamp tolerable? Will the lark need to do all dressing and grooming in the bathroom or is a bit of morning noise okay? Will either person need to use sleeping aids like earplugs and eye masks? This approach has some bonuses: you can take shifts with young kids if you have them, or use the gap in schedules to maintain interests and social circles your partner might not be interested in.

Aligning schedules is far trickier than the other options, but could bring a host of social and practical benefits. We're living in a lark's world, and couples who try this will gravitate to the lark's schedule, which aligns more with social patterns. Sorry, night owls – that means it's your body clock that's on notice.

Is it possible, or healthy, to realign your body clock? Some sleep specialists think not and warn that it's harmful to try.[85] Others suggest that chronotypes can be reset to a degree by getting back to nature and retraining the body by exposure to natural sunrise and sunset patterns.[86] Personally, I think it's possible to synchronise. My partner Juliana and I have done so. Juliana's a night owl but she's gradually adapted to my habits, not through force or effort but just because we choose to do the same things together. (Okay, I'll be honest – occasionally I pull the blinds up and force her out of bed with me in the mornings!)

The biological impulse for going to bed later is a genuine one for night owls, but it's often driven to exaggeration by a web of habits that can be reversed. Some late-night types aren't the real deal – they are 'social night owls', kept up by late-night gaming marathons or endless TV watching. If you are a suspected night owl who is burning the candle at both ends due to early starts at work or morning family demands, then nudging your body clock to an earlier bedtime is going to be a healthy move anyway, and adapting to your partner could provide motivation for new habits.

And the best way to get your clocks into alignment? Go camping together! Researchers took a mixed group of larks and night owls camping in Colorado, allowing them no access to electric lighting or torches. Within a week, all campers had synchronised their circadian rhythms and were rising at dawn![87]

A third solution is to sleep separately. This approach is on the rise among couples due to chronotype mismatch, snoring, body temperature discrepancies and even just a desire for more personal space. The US-based National Sleep Foundation puts figures at one in four couples now using separate rooms, while a Canadian survey reports a higher one in three.[88]

Some people view this 'sleep divorce' as evidence of relationship breakdown, or at least as a hindrance to both emotional and sexual intimacy.[89] But you don't need to sleep in the same room in order to have a healthy relationship.

Back to Carl and Louise. When they decided to move in together, they planned to share a room and work around each other's schedules. Both felt that sharing a bed was the 'right thing to do' for romantic partners, and both were willing to give it their best. As timing would have it, however, Carl injured his back just before the move and needed to be careful of his sleep set-up during recovery, so he took what was to be the spare room in their new two-bedroom nest.

It worked so well that they've never looked back. Many years later, the couple retains their separate bedroom policy (except during travel) and credits the strength of their relationship to good-quality sleep. The arrangement allows Louise, who runs her own business, to get up early and work, while Carl, who starts work later in the day, can respect his own body clock knowing that he's not disturbing his light-sleeping wife. The two spend plenty of time together and describe their marriage as healthy and close.

My mum and step-dad took this approach a step further and lived in separate houses! They loved each other very much, but didn't enjoy sharing a bedroom and decided to keep their own spaces. We spent plenty of time together as a family. My step-dad would turn up on the doorstep with flowers and whisk my mum out on dates, so in some ways I think this approach kept the spark in their relationship going strong, while other relationships succumb to the law of familiarity.

Their advice to other out-of-sync lovebirds? Stop worrying about what other people think. If space and money permit, then trial separate bedrooms – or separate houses! – and see what benefits it can bring to your relationship. If you communicate well and make opportunities for quality time together, then there's no need at all for intimacy to suffer. In fact, you may feel more able to maintain the romance when there's less blanket stealing, bad breath and sleep deprivation to contend with.

Maintaining the love

With things like snoring and out-of-sync body clocks, the toll they take on your sleep quality and intimate relationships is often obvious. But there are some more subtle undercurrents in our relationships that can come into play.

All of us go through phases of relationship drift. Over time, partners can lose a sense of appreciation for one another. Holding on to a sense of gratitude for each other is one of the hallmarks of couples who stay content in their relationships over the course of many years. On the other hand, loss of gratitude and appreciation between partners can jeopardise a relationship's long-term success.

Unsurprisingly, sleep can influence the emotional dynamic of a relationship. A study out of the University of California, Berkeley, suggests that poor sleep may contribute to a lack of appreciation between romantic partners. Sixty heterosexual couples were asked to make a gratitude list each morning for two weeks, naming five things they were grateful for. Researchers found that declining gratitude was connected with poor sleep, and sleep-deprived participants were more likely to describe themselves as selfish. Most interesting of all was that poor sleep in one partner impacted the mood of both partners: 'a lack of sleep by one person in the relationship resulted in greater likelihood of diminished feelings of appreciation by both partners.'[90]

But as with many aspects of the healthy sleep spiral, it's worth asking which comes first: the ungrateful chicken or the sleep-deprived egg? Emotional distance from a partner leads to a loss of intimacy and can make the confines of the bedroom a stressful place to be, leading to poor sleep outcomes. This is particularly true, it seems, if you're a woman. One study found that unhappily married women are 50% more likely to deal with insomnia than those in a happy marriage![91]

You're already working on the sleep side of things. But cultivating more appreciation is a great way to be proactive about stopping poor sleep in its tracks. Couples who work on new habits of expressing appreciation for each other both last longer and have deeper connections.[92] If you've already been feeling a bit of drift in the relationship department, whether due to poor sleep or anything else, growing some gratitude for your partner is a brilliant way to counterbalance that drift. If things are still rosy and intimate, then keep that vibe going with that gratitude attitude!

What is gratitude? It's not just saying thanks every now and then in response to a service or kindness, but respecting someone else's value, treasuring their uniqueness. We do this naturally in the early stages of relationships, but once the honeymoon phase has passed it's easy to take our partner for granted. Thankfully, even where the spark is lost, gratitude for each other can be regained.

Regaining gratitude could start as simply as writing down one thing you appreciate about your partner at night before bed. Even if you keep your thoughts in a private journal and don't share them with your partner, you'll be surprised how quickly this brings fondness to the relationship again. It's all about shifting your own perspective: as you look for the good in another person, you start to find it and honour it again.

Showing and telling your partner you appreciate them adds momentum – but not everyone hears or receives gratitude in the same way. I've found Gary Chapman's *The Five Love Languages* the hands-down best tool for learning how to show appreciation for people in ways that really hit the target.[93] Chapman argues that there are five different ways, or languages, in which people experience love. These are:

1. **Words of affirmation:** If this is your language, you're most sensitive to what's being said or left unsaid. Hearing that you're loved and appreciated is music to your ears, and being told why is even better. Insults can be damaging, and in your mind actions don't always speak louder than words.

2. **Quality time:** Do you thrive on the full and focused attention of another? Quality time types want everything else to go on hold in order to feel loved. Receiving undivided attention makes you feel valued and appreciated, whereas being brushed off, stood up or ignored in preference for a smartphone can really hurt.

3. **Acts of service:** Nothing says 'I love you' like cleaning the toilet – at least not to an 'acts of service' person! If this is you, then anyone who says 'let me take care of that for you' will have you feeding out of their hand. You feel loved and appreciated when your loved one takes care of things without prompting. Being taken for granted or left with the lion's share of work by a lazy partner crushes you.

4. **Receiving gifts:** If you feel known, understood and loved when you receive something thoughtful, this might be your love language. You're not materialistic so much as clued in to the intention and

effort behind a thoughtful gift or gesture. You feel unvalued when your birthday is overlooked, and uncared for when your loved one doesn't display care or effort in their gestures.

5. **Physical touch:** If presence, closeness and touch help you feel loved and appreciated, you're a 'physical touch' person. This isn't all about sex, but about feeling secure, accepted and cared for. Withdrawal, distance or absence from a loved one can really rock your boat.

Do you have any idea what your own primary love language is? Any idea what your partner's is? All of us have mixes of these gifts, and you can take an online survey to find out which language is dominant for you.[94] Knowing this stuff can take the way you express your gratitude to the next level while also helping to iron out those many small misunderstandings you have about your partner all the time.

This is especially the case when you speak a different love language to your partner. If you're an 'acts of service' person in a relationship with a 'quality time' person, for example, you might express love through practical actions – then feel unappreciated when it goes unnoticed. Meanwhile, your partner might even be resentful that you're so task-oriented that you couldn't be bothered to sit down and really talk to them. Knowing your own love languages and those of your partner go a long way to clearing up these kinds of misunderstandings.

Learning to express gratitude and love in a foreign language takes work. There have been times in the past where I haven't been so self-aware. My beautiful fiancée Juliana, she needs to hear 'I love you' every day. If she doesn't hear it, then I don't love her. My main love languages are acts of service and physical touch. Words mean almost nothing to me, so I have to work to make sure that she's feeling loved and adored.

The one that has ruined many relationships for me is gifts. I hate gifts. I hate receiving gifts. For me, when you give me a gift, I'm almost embarrassed because I have everything I need. If I need something, I'll buy it. But then, I've had partners in the past who needed gifts to feel appreciated, and I failed to understand that need.

Become skilled in 'cross-cultural communication' by learning the languages of your partner – and sharing your own with them, too. This is going to clear up so much conflict. You're going to feel loved. Your partner's going to feel loved. By understanding or mastering those languages, you can put a stop to that relationship drift – and reap the rewards of better sleep.

PART THREE

STRATEGIES FOR BETTER SLEEP

8. YOUR SANCTUARY

'Go to your room!'

'Not until you've tidied your room!'

'Finish your dinner or it's straight to bed for you!'

These near-universal phrases from childhood have played a role in cementing a negative view of the bedroom for many people, well into adulthood. The bedroom has retained these childhood overtones for many of us. It's seen as a room of isolation, punishment or boredom, and is neglected or avoided. Or we could still be treating it as a survival bunker like we did in our teenage years, and it remains a place to hide our stuff and our selves away from the rest of the household.

What's your bedroom like? What emotions does it evoke in you when you think about it? Does the thought of being in your bedroom make you feel calm, or does it bring a sense of heaviness and dread?

If you're someone who has a negative hangover from childhood about your bedroom space, you have a great opportunity now to undo these messages and to start thinking of your bedroom in a far more positive way. It's time to embrace your bedroom as the most important room in the house and transform it into a space that brings calm, ease and wellbeing – somewhere you love to be.

It's time to create your sleep haven. And your sleep haven has two key aspects: a relaxing environment and a supportive mattress.

A relaxing environment

If you're going to sleep well and grow healthy in the crazy, busy, strung-out twenty-first century, then you need to create your own oasis of calm. You need a bedroom environment that is set up to soothe and de-stress you.

This might seem self-indulgent. After all, generations of humans have got by just fine for centuries with the most rudimentary and temporary sleeping arrangements. In England in the Middle Ages, for example, whole villages would gather round in communal spaces, piling themselves around the fire on grass-stuffed hessian sacks with stumps of wood for pillows.

But in our time and culture, most of us have access to a private space designated for sleeping. The most recent census revealed that the average Australian household has 3.1 bedrooms and only 2.6 occupants, so we're not exactly squeezed for space![95] Of course, you might be co-sleeping with a partner, some children, a roommate or a whole menagerie of pets. But whether one, two or ten people are hitting the sack in the bedroom at night, the space you go to still needs to be a calm one.

If you've ever lived in student digs or awkward share house situations, then you'll have been through a phase when your bedroom was necessarily a multifunctional space: the place you'd go to study, entertain friends, avoid arguments about the washing-up roster, and watch your favourite TV show without the running commentary from that weird new housemate. It's not so different from the middleclass English bedchamber of the late 1600s, which, though a private bedroom of sorts, was also the occupant's main space for socialising and conducting business. (You can find paintings of Henry VIII holding court in his bedchamber. Perhaps this explains his relationship problems?)

But the bedroom is not a boardroom. It's not a media room. If you use your bedroom for work or entertainment, your mind will associate the space with activity and find it harder to switch off. A bedroom is your own private regeneration chamber. And it should be used for just two things: sleep and intimacy.[96]

The following steps will help you turn your bedroom into an oasis.

1. Keep it calm

The most crucial element in creating a calm bedroom environment is to keep your screens and tech devices out of the bedroom. We've already discussed the impact of blue electronic light on the quality of your sleep. LED light basically tricks your body into thinking it is daytime, triggering the untimely production of hormones such as cortisol, which is bad news for your circadian rhythm. To reverse the effects of this damaging light, sleep experts now recommend finishing up screen use at least ninety minutes before bedtime, which will allow your melatonin levels to recalibrate.

You may want to object to this restriction of your perceived screen freedom. Perhaps you use your phone as your alarm clock? If so, it's time to invest in an old-school alarm clock or, better yet, allow yourself to wake up naturally. Because, alongside the blue light issues and potential for disruption by pesky telemarketers in other time zones, sleeping next to your smartphone – a microcosm of every single thing you're responsible for in your life – is simply not a habit conducive to deep relaxation.

What if you like to read on your phone or tablet? There are plenty of other more brain-soothing options – like paper books, for example! But if you absolutely must, then do yourself a favour and use a blue light blocker, either in app form or in the form of glasses.

Beyond blue light, there might be other forms of light pollution cramping your circadian style. Sleeping in total darkness is best for our melatonin production. Switch your main room bulb to a warm, low-energy mood light. When it's lights-out time, make sure any cracks of light from outside the room can be blocked off, and cover any standby lights on remaining electronic devices. If you're someone who needs a nightlight, try a soft red light, like the gentle glow of a Himalayan salt lamp, as this will have far less impact on your body clock than other forms of light.

After light pollution, noise pollution is the second biggest disruptor. Much of this depends on your own state of arousal and just how much noise bothers you. For some people, nearby traffic becomes a soothing part of their sleep backdrop, while for others it becomes a trigger for sleeplessness.

If you're in this situation, do what you can to insulate your bedroom. This could mean actually insulating the walls and floor against outside noise, or simply bringing in more soft furnishings to dampen and absorb noise. Beyond that, invest in a set of decent earplugs!

2. Keep it clean

Where do you fall on a scale of 'neat freak' to 'pack rat'? In your bedroom, are all your clothes up and away, or have they lived on the floor for so long that you've forgotten the colour of the carpet and you're ready to trademark the term 'floordrobe'?

A disorganised, cluttered room can contribute to stress and anxiety, making it more difficult for you to drift off. Making a habit of tidying up before bed is not only a good general life skill but will also help you sleep better. You don't have to do a deep clean every day, just make sure walking into your bedroom doesn't immediately stress you out. Put your clothes in the wardrobe, papers in the drawer, and (this message has been sponsored by your significant other) please stop hoarding mugs.

Removing unnecessary furnishings and giving the place a soothing and unifying colour scheme are other great ways to bring a fresh and clean feel to your bedroom. One fascinating study in the UK found that people who sleep in blue bedrooms get the best rest, while those in purple or brown bedrooms are seriously underdoing their sleep.[97] It could be time to take a look at your colour palette and opt for a more calming tone.

Keeping your bed linen fresh and clean is another obvious way to keep the room clean, but don't forget about your pillow! Given that it cradles your head for so many hours of the day, your pillow holds all kinds of nasties – fungus, bacteria and dead skin cells, to name a few. I don't want to freak you out, but by the time your pillow is two years old, a tenth of its weight is from skin cells and dust mite poo![98] It's recommended that you change your pillow at least every two years in order to keep things healthy.

Finally, air quality is another thing to consider. If you can, get some fresh air into your bedroom in the evening before you sleep. Stale air can get smelly and unpleasant, to say the least. It also loses its negative ions, which oxidise odours and chemicals and bind to dust and pollen, making them easier to remove. If investing in an air ioniser sounds a bit too 'woo' for you, then add an indoor plant to your bedroom. Plants purify the air and bring a sense of calm and joy – as long as you're not allergic or overly stressed out by tending to them.

3. Keep it cool

As bedtime approaches, your core temperature naturally drops and remains lowered throughout the time you're asleep. A cooler bedroom – ideally around 18 °C – helps facilitate this temperature drop. If your sleep environment is much hotter than 18 °C, you're more likely to have trouble falling and staying asleep.

There are a couple of benefits to 'sleeping cool'. One is that the healthy temperature regulation during sleep helps keep cortisol levels on an even keel. A second is that people who sleep in cooler environments have better weight regulation, with double the amount of healthy brown fat compared to those who sleep in hotter rooms.

Sleeping in a room that's too warm, even if it feels cosy initially, can mess with your body's thermoregulation and keep you tossing and turning. If you 'sleep hot' you're going to be more stressed, possibly fatter, and as a kicker your body will also have less ability to regulate temperature during the daytime. So it's worth figuring out how you can keep your bedroom climate on the cooler side!

Beyond air conditioning and fans, one suggestion is to sleep in the nude. Being in the buff helps your body regulate temperature and cool down naturally as you drift off to sleep. Pyjamas tend to hold your body temperature at a level that hinders your dip into REM sleep.

Exercise: Audit your sleep sanctuary

1. Do an audit of your current bedroom set-up.

    On a scale of 1 to 10:

    How calm is it?

    How clean is it?

    How cool is it?

2. Which area is contributing most to a healthy bedroom environment? Which area needs immediate attention?

3. List three actions you can take to make your bedroom calmer, cooler and cleaner right now.

A supportive bed

Your mattress matters.

I say 'mattress' rather than 'bed', because the choices around bed base, material, height and style are largely aesthetic ones. So many people get caught up on whether to get slats or an ensemble or obsess over bedhead versus under-bed storage, when the real questions should focus on the main equipment.

Your mattress is, unequivocally, the most used piece of furniture in your home. In my family we have a saying: the two most important things you can invest in are a good pair of shoes and a good mattress. During the day you're on your feet; at night you're on your back.

Think of the number of hours you spend lying on your mattress over a lifetime: that mattress will outdo any chair, any lounge suite, any motorbike or car seat. So, if the mattress isn't well-engineered and designed, or you've just been on the same one too long and it's no longer supportive, then you're putting your body into a suboptimal posture for eight hours every day. That's going to take a toll on your physical health. It's like slouching at your desk for eight continuous hours, hoping there'll be no negative effect. Try it right now – find an uncomfortable chair, hunch down and stick your neck forward. Horrible, right? Nobody would stay in that position voluntarily for eight hours. Yet you might be putting yourself into a horrible position, night after night, and doing yourself a real disservice.

Want to know whether your current mattress is doing its job? A good test is how you feel in the first ten minutes after getting up in the morning. A lot of people feel stiff. A lot of people feel sore. A lot of people need a hot shower to get going. Frankly, that's not how you should feel after a high quality, uninterrupted, restful night's sleep in optimal posture, on a supportive mattress, with an appropriate pillow.

What makes a good mattress? We're spoilt for choice these days with a great range of shapes, styles and sizes in a wide range of materials. Our Neolithic relatives slept on piles of dirt and leaves, the Egyptians opted for palm branches, and even our Renaissance forebears were still quite literally 'hitting the hay', sleeping on sacks stuffed with grass and pea shucks. Let's be grateful that our bedding options have evolved alongside us!

Here are the main features of a great mattress:

1. Support

Different materials support the body in different ways. Memory foam contours to your body and absorbs movement. Latex is similar, but has more firmness and resistance, so will push back against your body to provide support. The coils in an innerspring mattress contract to different depths depending on your sleeping position.

Pocket spring systems are widely acknowledged to be the market leader now – all the top mattress providers sell them. In a queen size bed this system provides about 750 springs – far more than the basic Bonnell spring system (which I suggest you save for your mother-in-law when she visits). More springs equals more support – it's that simple.

First, the high spring count. More springs equals more support, and more support is going to improve your outcomes. Think about lying on a bed of nails. If you have 100 nails under your body, you're going to feel every single individual nail. If you're on a bed with 3,000 nails, you're going to feel more support over the entire body. Now obviously springs aren't as sharp and painful as nails, but you get the picture! Ask your mattress provider to show you their range of highest spring count mattresses straight up. At Regal, we've created a pocket spring mattress with 2,250 springs in queen size. This one, called the Healthy Life mattress, gives such excellent support that it is now classed by Australia's Therapeutic Goods Administration as a grade 1 medical device.

Alongside a high spring count, check that the system gives you longer springs. These provide better pressure relief. It's like the suspension in a car. Your four-wheel drive has bigger suspension coils than a normal sedan, so you feel fewer bumps in the road. Longer springs in a mattress mean a less bumpy night's sleep!

2. Zoning

A mistake people make when looking for a supportive mattress is to opt for the stiffest, firmest mattress they try, assuming that this means 'support'. However, a truly supportive mattress will also provide some fluidity, allowing some parts of your body to sink in a bit further.

A zoned pocket spring system works like an orthotic for your feet. Zoning places softer or firmer springs at different points in the mattress to correspond to your shoulder, hips, lumbar and lower back regions, allowing your hips and shoulders to sink in further and achieve a neutral spine. The hips and shoulders are the heaviest parts of the body, so they need softer springs to allow them to sink more deeply, helping you maintain a nice, neutral spine position all night long.

As Dr Michael Haworth, chiropractor and postural expert, says, 'You need a mattress that is designed for the human shape, because, let's face it, most mattresses are all the exact same spring rate, all lined up, perfectly uniform – designed for rectangles.'

But with fluidity, you also want to minimise disturbance. Even if you're not a really restless sleeper, you will often move throughout the night as your body prompts you to shift away from pressure points in order to improve blood flow and avoid pressure sores. Pocket springs are once again the best for this, as the high number of springs and the pocketing around them stop what we call 'partner disturbance'. That means if you're chasing rabbits in your sleep, you won't wake Sleeping Beauty on the other side of the bed (and this is good thing for your relationship!)

3. A firm edge

Finally, you want your mattress to have great edge support. This means that it needs firmer springs around the perimeter of the mattress. A firm-edged mattress allows you to lever yourself in and out of bed safely and comfortably. It's particularly important for people with sore necks, backs or shoulders, or any kind of injury, to get themselves in and out of the bed easily and with good support.

Firm edges also extend the life of your mattress. Like me, you probably sit at the edge of your bed to put your shoes and socks on. If you're doing that several times a day on a regular soft-edged mattress, you'll start to notice the edge sag far too early in its life.

4. Comfort

Beyond support, zoning and firm edges, comfort comes down more to personal preference. You can top your pocket spring mattress with either memory foam or latex, receiving the benefits of whichever material you prefer without experiencing the drawbacks of mattresses made solely from those materials. For latex-only mattresses, these drawbacks can include excessive firmness, too much bounce and lack of edge support, whereas foam-only mattresses often suffer from a lack of breathability and deteriorate more quickly.

You want a foam that will not break down quickly. Lower density foams will feel soft and comfy initially, so you might be tempted for something softer at first, but higher-density foams minimise body impressions and will last far longer.

Be on the lookout for premium grade, high-density foam that will last the test of time. What's more, go for a locally made product. Foams produced overseas are often treated with harsh chemicals – around 80 per cent of Chinese foams, for example, are treated with formaldehyde, and who wants to be breathing that in night after night? I partner with Foamco, a fantastic Australian foam manufacturing business, to get the best local foams for my mattresses. These foams are premium grade, made with approved chemicals and glues, and produced in environmentally qualified facilities, all of which is vital for your health.

Buying your mattress

The best thing to do is go out to a mattress showroom and try before you buy. Tempting and convenient as an online purchase might seem, it's far wiser to get a genuine feel for the product you're about to invest in. Go somewhere where you can get personal and specific advice, and be taught about healthy sleep postures and best practice in sleep hygiene. That's what I train my staff to provide, and it's so much more helpful than an impersonal online purchase.

Knowing the four key things you're after in a mattress – support, fluidity, comfort and a firm edge –will simplify the process a whole lot. Here are a few more tips to help make the process as straightforward as possible.

1. Shop when you're calm

When you're calm you're going to make a better decision, ask good questions and feel less pressured. A mattress is a big investment of your money. You don't want to make an impulse purchase; unlike that pair of unnecessary shoes, a mattress is going to be hard to stuff at the back of the wardrobe!

Two things that will ease your purchase stress are decent warranty agreements and a money-back guarantee. Mattress providers who are proud of their product quality will offer both and will bend over backwards to make sure you get the right mattress for you. This provides great reassurance of product quality as well as taking the pressure out of your financial commitment.

2. Take your time

I can't stress this enough. When you go to test a mattress, you need to genuinely test it.

Okay, so you don't need to turn up in your pyjamas and bring your bedtime reading. But you (and your partner) do need to come prepared to spend at least ten minutes on any mattress you're interested in. You want time to get a feel for the bed's support and zoning as well as try out a few different padding and fibre options.

I suggest bringing your current pillow along to try out. Not only does this avoid hygiene issues, it will also help you focus on the difference the mattress makes first. If you try out a new pillow at the same time, you may be distracted or confused by the pillow feel and not able to focus on how the bed itself feels.

3. Upgrade your pillow

However, once you're happy with the mattress choice, take the time to consider how supportive (and old!) your pillow is.

The main role of your pillow is to support neck and shoulder alignment. You'll want something that nestles into your neck and maintains the right gap between your head and the mattress, keeping your head and neck in the same kind of alignment with your spine as they hold when you're upright.

Once again, trial and error is going to be your friend here, as there are pros and cons to each material style and firmness. Postural support is the key issue, and it's worth seeking a recommendation from your chiropractor, osteopath or physiotherapist, who will know your own unique needs.

4. Don't pay too much

A good mattress is expensive. If it's well-engineered, the materials are good quality and the craftsmanship is of a high calibre, the price will reflect that. And it's worth your investment, given it's something that will last you ten years or more.

But it shouldn't be *too* expensive. Don't be afraid to ask any mattress supplier the hard questions about their materials. Who designed the mattress? Has it been tested? Where are the materials sourced? Where is the mattress made? What components add to its expense? Why is this model a different price from that model? Is this mattress recommended by any reputable sources not directly connected to the supplier?

For a good-quality pocket spring mattress, you can pay anywhere between $1,000 and $4,000. Unless you're a professional athlete who needs something more that is specifically designed for you with materials like copper and silk, then you don't need to be paying more than that. If you see price tags up over $10,000, get out of there. There's simply no reason for a mattress to cost you that much money.

5. Trial for a few weeks

Finally, once you've decided on a mattress and have taken your new best friend home, be sure to give yourself time to adjust. Unless there's a fault or product failure that becomes quickly apparent, any new mattress is likely to feel unfamiliar for a week or two. This is particularly the case for people whose systems are already on edge from lack of sleep and whose senses are hyper-alert to all changes in environment.

But if you're not feeling at all comfortable after two to four weeks, it's time to make use of that money-back guarantee. If you like the people you are dealing with, try swapping over to a different model. It may be that you discover an allergy issue that didn't arise in the showroom, or that you just made the wrong choice for your body. These are understandable issues and shouldn't be worn by the customer. Any mattress company that values customer service will help you resolve the issue, or provide you with a full refund if necessary.

With a new calming environment and a supportive mattress, your bedroom is set to become your own private regeneration chamber. Move over, health spa, sauna and flotation tank – the bedroom is where it's at for healthy living. Any lingering negative associations from earlier in life will fade away. Even just thinking about your bedroom will bring you into a state of ease and relaxation. And best of all, your sleep will become the rejuvenating experience you deserve.

9. YOUR ROUTINE

Human beings thrive on routine.

Routine – we use it as a synonym for bland, boring and predictable. And no one wants to be those things. We like to think we're exciting and surprising types.

But as much as we tell ourselves that variety is the spice of life and spontaneity is where it's at, the reality is that true freedom is underpinned by patterns, habits and rituals. A lead singer in a band can't rock out if the drums and bass are all over the place – the performance will fall apart. In the same way, a life of chaos can't support you in the great things you want to do.

The fact that we're routine-based beings becomes obvious as soon as you consider the marvel that is the circadian clock. This clock wants us to stay in sync with it and lets us know it's not happy when we disrespect it. Jet lag is the obvious example: if you travel far enough to experience time zone alteration, your body gets very confused. Your sleep is disturbed, your digestion is off and you may even get headaches.

More positively, studies are showing that working *with* your body clock can improve your health outcomes and optimise things like productivity and performance. For example, many sports coaches are realising the competitive edge that might be gained by working with athletes' circadian rhythms and particular chronotypes.[99] While a sports coach can't dictate when a game or performance takes place, they can tailor training schedules to an athlete's peak activity window in the daytime, which allows for better performance gains and adaptions.

Finding a sleep routine is all about honouring that internal rhythm and respecting your own body clock. A healthy sleep routine is going to involve both a clear sleep schedule to get your sleep quantity consistent, and a scaffolding of habits and rituals to deepen sleep quality.

Setting your schedule

Are you someone who likes to use weekends and holidays to catch up on sleep? I have bad news for you.

Catching up on sleep is a myth.

Some of us treat our sleep schedule as though we're on a month-by-month 'sleep plan' with rollover credit: if you don't use it it's no big deal, because you'll have some extra sleep hours up your sleeve for that week-long sleep binge during your next holiday, right?

Wrong. Your 'sleep plan' renews every twenty-four hours. There is no rollover. If you don't use it, you lose it.

Sure, if you're out a little late one night and can balance that with a sleep-in the next morning, that's a sensible tactic. But if you're skimming off hours of sleep during your weekday (perhaps by staying up late to get extra work done or getting up early to go the gym), you're not repaying that debt when you crash for twelve hours straight over the weekend. It's simply not how the body clock works.

This is why it's so important to get out of the 'I'll catch it up later' mentality and set a regular sleep schedule. Researchers at the University of Arizona have shown that this kind of fluctuating schedule, which they term 'social jetlag', has significantly poorer outcomes in heart health, mood and fatigue levels than a consistent schedule.[100] What's more, the results were independent of how much sleep the participants got, *and* whether they had any insomnia symptoms! Clearly, restrict-and-binge patterns of sleeping are damaging to your health.

A health-promoting sleep schedule is one that will see you waking at around the same time every morning of the week, and going to bed around the same time every evening of the week, in accordance with your own particular circadian rhythm.

The best way to set yourself a consistent sleep schedule is to select a wake-up time and use it every morning of the week, including weekends. According to sleep specialist Dr Chris Winter, this is the keystone habit for all good sleep schedules, because the right wake-up time dictates both how your daily routine will flow and when your ideal bedtime needs to be. As for what that time should be, Dr Winter says there is no such thing as a bad wake-up time. Your personal wake-up time simply needs to take into account your practical needs – work hours, time for commuting, grooming and exercise, family needs and life admin – and your own body clock preferences.[101]

One way forward is to wake up around the same time in order to send the right body signals, but then return to bed for a lie-in with the papers. Physiotherapist Jason Smith, who gets up regularly by 6am on workdays, takes this approach, keeping roughly similar hours but taking out the gym visit and relaxing the surrounding routine on Saturdays and Sundays.

Setting a sleep schedule sounds simple, but can be far from easy. You could be someone whose body clock preference screams 'night owl' but career choice screams '5am alarm', so you burn the candle at both ends. You could be one of the hundreds of thousands of exhausted parents who, after putting their little darlings to bed at night, crave adult time so badly that they stay up way too late into the evening and hit the snooze button multiple times in the morning, or sleep in shifts around little Johnny's midnight rave sessions. You could have a crazily varied morning routine based around your hobbies: you get up 5:30am on Mondays for boot camp, but sleep in on Friday after Thursday night's indoor soccer game. Worst of all, you could be a shiftworker.

If you fall into one of the first three camps, it's time to take the ill effects of social jet lag seriously and start to standardise your schedule. This could mean you'll have to knuckle through a time of disciplined change.

A little while ago I was inspired by retired United States Navy SEAL Jocko Willink and his book, *Discipline Equals Freedom*.[102] Jocko's approach to waking up early in the morning is simply to own that sucker. He sees the alarm clock as a test that sets the tone for the rest of the day. If you get up to the alarm, you pass the test; if you don't, you fail. 'It's not fun to get out of bed early in the morning. When the alarm goes off, it doesn't sing you a song, it hits you in the head with a baseball bat. So how do you respond to that? Do you crawl underneath your covers and hide? Or do you get up, get aggressive, and attack the day?'[103]

Thanks to Jocko Willink, my wake-up time these days is 4:55am, an hour I used to consider ungodly (unless I hadn't gone to bed yet, in which case it was heroic). I've been re-energised to be more committed to my morning exercise routine. I'm asleep by 10.30pm – and I'm now inching that back to 9–9.30pm. My team members at work actually laugh. They call me grandpa, but they no longer try to call me late at night because they know I'm out dead.

Exercise: Set your sleep schedule

Write down your current weekly sleep schedule, noting day-to-day variations. How much does your schedule change each day? How wide is the variation between weekday and weekend wake-up times?

What consistent wake-up time would fit best across your whole week? Working backwards seven to nine hours, what time should you go to bed to achieve enough sleep on this schedule? Write these down.

What regular activities or habits are you willing to reconsider to get a consistent bedtime? What alternatives do you have? What supports will you need to change these?

Commit to trying your new wake-up time for the next month:

- **Week 1:** concentrate on rising to your alarm, especially at the weekend. Set as many alarms as you need. Don't concern yourself with bedtimes yet.

- **Week 2:** stay focused on rising to your alarm. How is it working for your weekly schedule? What time are you gravitating towards bed? Adjust your wake-up time if necessary.

- **Week 3:** keep going with your morning alarm, and set a clearer bedtime seven to nine hours earlier based on last week's experiences.

- **Week 4:** Consolidate!

Schedules for shiftworkers

Now to return to the peskiest of all issues: shiftwork. Perhaps you are one of the 1.5 million Australians working in transport, hospitality, mining, protective services or health whose main job involves work that begins and/or ends outside of daylight hours. Shiftworkers are statistically more likely to be obese, have diabetes and suffer from poor mental health and chronic pain. They are also at higher risk for workplace and road accidents.[104]

If shiftwork is part of your reality, then you're constantly butting up against your circadian rhythm. If you work rotating shifts it's particularly challenging to find a routine. There's no possibility of standardising the wake-up time or aiming for a regular bedtime. And, apart from the lack of regularity, you also face the temptation to skip sleep to maintain a social life with non-shift-working pals or get things done during regular business hours. Even though you know you should be heading home for dinner and bed, it's hard to do when the world is just getting out for morning coffee and life is buzzing around you.

But the harmful effects of a rotating roster can be minimised. Establishing a 'moveable routine' that keeps the same pre-bed rituals and wake-up patterns will help. Grooming, eating proper meals, exercising, socialising and relaxing in as normal a fashion as possible around each shift will send the right cues to your brain.

You also need to outwit your circadian pacemaker to some extent. To do so, the clever use of light is going to be your best friend. Phototherapy, or exposure to artificial light to simulate daytime, has great potential for helping your body clock move with ease into your 'daytime' phase. Investing in a therapy light box or some goggles could be the right thing for you.

Light *avoidance* is the key to simulating the evening wind-down and telling your body it's bedtime. Switch off those screens a few hours before bedtime to allow your brain to start producing melatonin – or, if you're going to look at a phone or tablet, at least use a red light filter. To keep the daytime light and noise out of your bedroom, blackout curtains are your friend. If this is impractical, learn to love your eye mask and earplugs. And don't feel like you need to put up with the cheap ones you get on a long-haul flight – there are some amazing eye masks available these days especially for shiftworkers.

Finally, you could investigate getting a prescription for melatonin supplements. Melatonin is not a sedative, but rather a synthetic version of the hormone your body produces, and it's used to reset the circadian rhythm. The jury is still out on its effectiveness for shiftwork: there's some evidence that it doesn't improve a shiftworker's sleep quality, or the time it takes them to fall asleep, but does alleviate daytime fatigue.[105] The good news is that it is a safe form of supplement to try, so it's worth trialling alongside the phototherapy. One friend of mine who works in intensive care nursing finds it very effective to take melatonin when she's transitioning from late shifts or overnights to early, and vice versa. It kick-starts the new schedule for her, but then she finds her body gets with the program and she lets her routine carry her.

These tricks will be enough to keep you away from the stimulant-and-sedative cycle many shiftworkers fall into. Remember, sedation does not equal sleep – only genuine shut-eye will help you feel truly rested. As for stimulants, a bit of coffee to perk you up is fine, but don't fall for the hype of energy drinks and supplements. A happy hormonal system is enough to 'give you wings'!

Healthy supporting habits

In order to support your schedule and cement it into your routine, add some habits and rituals that will encourage better sleep.

By habits, I mean ingrained and automatic actions. A habit is something you perform unthinkingly. Here's the thing – you already have a bunch of habits that impact on your sleep. They just might not be good ones! Do you check social media on your phone last thing before your head hits the pillow? Do you always unwind with a nightcap or a bowl of ice-cream late in the evening? Do you spend the last half hour before bed making urgent work calls or trying to get emails out ahead of the working day? These are habits and, whether you've thought about it this way or not, they form part of your sleep routine, cueing your body for a disrupted night.

Poor habits can be hard to remove – but they can be gradually displaced. It's far more fun and rewarding to focus first on adding small, positive steps towards good sleep than it is to weed out all the nasties. The bonus is that these new habits will then begin to squeeze out the old. As you begin to feel calmer about sleep, you will look forward to your relaxing bedtime and wake-up routines. Your attachment to less helpful habits will begin to loosen. Your identity will shift and these older habits won't have quite the pull they used to, because you are no longer the 'phone junkie' or the 'stressed out self-soother' or the 'control freak' but the relaxed, balanced person you've been wanting to become.

In the case of a good habit, getting to the point of unthinking automation is a wonderful thing. When we become competent at something at an unconscious level, it frees up space to do other things in our lives. We have a limited amount of willpower and discipline. When we constantly draw on willpower to perform tasks, our 'willpower muscle' starts to fatigue. When we have to consciously choose to do something, we get 'decision fatigue'. Automation means you can save your limited willpower and decision-making energies for the things that really need it. Early in my working life I decided to give myself a work uniform of sorts so I didn't have to think about what to wear every day. For the past eighteen years, for example, I've been working in white shirts and black pants or suits. All my work clothes work together, and I love not having to put energy into clothing decisions every morning. It keeps my brain free for things that are more important to me.

What is the difference between a habit and a ritual? Sometimes rituals and habits can look the same and involve the same actions, but here's a way to think about the distinction: a habit is an action you perform for its own sake, while a ritual is an action, or string of actions, that you engage in to create a mood or bring meaning and significance to your life. So the ultimate difference is not necessarily the action itself, but the intention behind the action. Intentionality is key.

Take drinking a glass of water. That's an action you undertake without too much thought – maybe a glass with every meal, or just when you're thirsty. It's probably second nature to you to reach for the tap as you walk into the kitchen at the end of the day, or when your mouth is feeling a little dry. This is something you do it for its own sake: to quench thirst and stay hydrated.

But when you drink a glass of water as part of a set of wake-up actions, it becomes ritualised and takes on greater meaning beyond mere hydration. It is now a cue for your body and mind to begin the day in a replenished state. It may even become symbolic of something deeper, like approaching the new day clean and fresh, or with clear and fluid thinking. If you want to take your good sleep habits to the next level, make them part of a ritual.

Below are a few tried and true habits of the sleep masters that could become part of your morning or evening rituals.

Upon waking…

Drink a glass of water. You breathe out water vapour all night without replenishing it. Even if your body isn't telling you that it's thirsty in the morning, it probably is. Before you eat anything, drink a cup or two of water to hydrate your cells and fire up your metabolism. You'll feel refreshed and energetic, and your brain will feel more sharp and clear. Keeping yourself hydrated is one of the best ways to keep your energy levels up no matter how much you've slept.

Expose yourself to natural light. Early exposure to natural light will suppress melatonin production, which is what you want at the start of the day. If you tend to wake up feeling groggy, it will likely help to step outside and spend a few minutes in the sun. Even opening the blinds and looking out the window should do the trick. Your body will clue into the fact that it's daytime, which should perk up your mood and energy levels. (Tip for shiftworkers: if you need to get up well before the sun, here's where it may be worth investing in a commercial therapy bulb that simulates natural light.)

Exercise first up. Getting your blood going in the morning will go a long way towards keeping you alert for the rest of the day. There's no need to stress yourself out with strenuous exercise, but a spot of yoga, a brisk walk or a good stretch will give you a natural high. I know someone who performs two minutes of body weight exercises – things like jumping jacks and lunges – after getting up. He can't get to the gym until much later on most days, so he does this to get his blood pumping a little. He also swears that this little routine kicks his brain into gear better than a shot of coffee used to do. (I say, why not have both?)

Add mindfulness meditation. Many people think of meditating as 'emptying the mind', and might associate it more with a winding down activity to help you go to sleep. But 'mindfulness' is a type of awareness training that is not about trying to stop your thoughts, but to learn to observe them and let them come and go without judgement. Mindfulness is a proven antidote to anxiety, and it's therefore a good skill to practise in the morning. The less anxious and hyper-alert your mind is during the day, the more easily it will succumb to sleep at night. I've been using an app called Headspace, which is a fantastic way to learn this style of awareness training.

And before bed...

Tidy your bedroom. There's nothing like the feeling of waking up in a clean, organised space. Fold that laundry, put the graveyard of tea mugs to rest in the dishwasher, and make sure everything is more or less in its place. You'll thank yourself when you don't have to scramble for matching socks in the morning.

Get ahead of your workday. If there are easy things you can do at night to shave a few minutes off your morning routine, do them. Plan your outfit and prep whatever part of breakfast you can ahead of time. These little tasks really add up in the early hours. This works particularly well for cueing a new exercise habit. Lay out your running gear right next to your bed – I do this every morning – or over the other side of your room, under the alarm clock!

Take a hot bath. A hot bath aids sleep by lowering your core body temperature – counterintuitive but true. This happens as your blood vessels dilate and radiate inner heat. Your core temperature needs to drop about one degree Celsius in order to initiate sleep. I just had a hot tub installed for this purpose. It's amazing.

Dim your household lights. We've covered plenty about the blue light from screens, but your household lights are another form of light pollution that disrupts your circadian clock. Dr Michael Haworth says that, while yellow halogen lighting is probably the best for our brains, halogen lamps aren't very efficient. So when going for LED lighting, look for lights with lower 'light temperature', measured in Kelvins (K). Go for warm lights with lower Kelvin: for example, something that is around 3,000 and is more of a sunset colour will be far less damaging to your sleep cycle than a 7,000 Kelvin light, which will be cool and bright blue. Save the cool lighting for workrooms and garages, and the warmer tones for indoors. Alongside this, the simple act of dimming your household lights when evening comes can really calm down your visual acuity and prepare your body for sleep. Turn off overhead lights, switch on the side-table lamps and some mood music, and you'll be in wind-down mode in no time.

Bury your nose in a book. Reading to put yourself to sleep is a time-honoured tradition. Plenty of research backs up the idea that reading improves cognitive function and lowers stress levels, so it makes all the sense in the world to make reading – if only for ten or fifteen minutes – a part of your bedtime routine. Even better, if you make reading before bed a consistent habit, it will help signal to your brain that it's time for sleep (like putting a towel over a bird cage). But make sure you don't read anything too exciting, or you brain might go into overdrive instead of settling down.

Keep a journal. Have a nagging issue you just can't get a handle on? Try writing down whatever's keeping you up at night (on a piece of paper, not your smartphone notepad), folding it up, and putting it away in your bedside drawer till the morning. This signals to your mind that the problem is off the table for the time being, helping to keep it from ricocheting around your brain. Or keep a gratitude journal and write down three things you're grateful for every night before you go to sleep. Neuroscientists have shown that regular gratitude practice literally changes the brain (but it takes about three months for the practice to have a lasting effect).[106]

Exercise: Run a routine audit

1. **Describe your current rituals and routines in the morning and evening.** Are there any parts of these that don't benefit your sleep?

2. **Which of the habits here appeal to you as a way to support your sleep schedule?** Can you think of something not listed here that might encourage better wake or sleep routines in your household?

3. **Pick one thing to add to your morning or evening routine this coming week.** Practise it consistently, and at the end of the week assess whether it's been worthwhile. What have you noticed? Has anything changed? Does going to bed feel any different? Will you keep this habit going?

Small habits might feel insignificant or ineffective, like the loose change in your pocket that seems worthless. But if you keep all of those loose coins and pool them together, after a while they add up to something. Before you know it, your coin jar savings can buy you a nice meal out with your friends (unless it's all gone into the swear jar).

One of the habits that has changed my life is taking a bit of time to practise a morning routine I learnt from Tony Robbins called 'three to thrive'. This routine primes me with a great mindset that carries on through my day, and when my day is great it's so much easier to rest well at night.

Set up your schedule, surround it with supportive habits, and you're well on your way to a better night's sleep.

10. YOUR DREAM TEAM

You're at the pointy end of the *Sleep and Grow Healthy* journey. Congratulations for making it through this far. On the way, you've picked up lots about the art of sleep. You've grown in your understanding of your own sleep patterns. Your knowledge has grown and you're even dropping terms like 'circadian rhythm', 'melatonin' and 'chronotype' into everyday conversation.

Now it's time to put that knowledge into action. Lots of the stuff in this book you can go ahead and implement yourself – and I want to encourage you to do just that. But for some of the thornier issues, perhaps you are looking for a nudge to get you going.

Most of the time we can only get so far on our own. Having a support network helps us to get further. Asking for help doesn't demonstrate any weakness on your part. In fact, seeking support is a sign that you're invested in your goals and ready to succeed.

Think of the most successful people you know out there – athletes, musicians, business people. The vast majority of them have mentors and coaches.[107] They have people who are on their side, providing direction and motivation, helping to plan and execute strategies, celebrating successes and navigating disappointments.

In this chapter we'll look at some of the professionals who work in wellness, health care and personal growth who can provide support to you in your quest for better sleep. But you're not looking for a sleep guru or saviour – you're looking for a coach.

Some people aren't used to viewing health practitioners through a 'coaching' lens. In their minds, health providers are only worth checking in with when you're desperately sick or broken in some way. They're for crisis intervention – like taking your car to the mechanic after a crash.

But think about it. You should also take your car to the mechanic during the year for a service. A good mechanic will provide you with routine maintenance that will prevent vehicle wear and tear, as well as improving your car's performance and longevity. A great mechanic will also educate you about how to take better care of your sweet ride yourself so you're not reliant on service visits. If you don't know how to check the oil and water, they'll show you, and they'll guide you on how to handle the quirks of your particular vehicle.

Your health team are not just there to patch you up in a crisis, but to coach you to take charge of your own healthy life. They will guide you to set your own goals, identify and overcome resistance, take responsibility for your own wellbeing and embrace a life of wellness and vitality.

What kind of modality is the best fit for you? That all depends on the core health concerns you've identified. We'll look at what sleep specialists can do, then at some of the supporting cast who can help with the broader web of habits your sleep is linked to.

The traditional route: getting a sleep study

If you've identified a potential sleep issue like obstructive sleep apnea, chronic insomnia or snoring, visit your GP for a referral to a sleep clinic, where you can get an overnight sleep study or polysomnography. This may help to pin down the source of your sleep problems.

What happens when you go for a sleep study? Before it starts, you may be asked to fill out a sleep questionnaire that tracks your sleep habits over a period of time. You'll probably be asked to bring your own pyjamas and any personal sleep objects to the study since these may help you sleep better (this is no time to be shy about that stuffed bunny rabbit you still sleep with).

Sleeping overnight in a laboratory may seem nerve-wracking, and many people wonder how they'll be able to get to sleep at all under such unusual conditions. Keep in mind that sleep labs are designed to be as comfortable as possible. Rarely does a sleep study fail because the patient couldn't get to sleep. And just to reassure you: there are no known risks associated with sleep studies, except mild skin irritation where the electrodes are attached. Oh, and mild embarrassment from being seen cuddling your Bunny-Wunny.

A sleep study uses precise measuring equipment to track your brain, muscle and eye activity, which together reveal the sleep stage you're in. Pauses in breathing, frequency of sleep arousals and intermittent drops in levels of oxygen in the blood will all help determine the type and severity of your sleep disorder and appropriate treatment.

After your study, a sleep specialist will discuss your results with you, potentially offer a diagnosis and then educate you about options for treatment. Your sleep study is most likely going to pick up – or rule out – obstructive sleep apnea, parasomnias (which are some of the more exotic sleep disorders including night terrors, night paralysis and sleepwalking) or insomnia.

If you have a cut-and-dried sleep apnea diagnosis, then you can expect to have CPAP and weight loss recommended. If you have hard insomnia that isn't responding to lifestyle and sleep hygiene changes, you'll be encouraged to see a sleep psychologist. For other trickier sleep arousal disorders generated within the brain, medications are often the main treatment on offer.

A sleep study is going to provide you and your health team with loads of useful information about what's going on overnight for you. But it's just the beginning of your path to sleep nirvana. Don't expect that all the hard work is over once the last electrode is removed, or that your sleep issue will be easily resolved.

To remain the master of your own sleep destiny, you will need to look beyond machines and medications and take a holistic approach to your problems.

Beyond the sleep study: who does what?

While sleep specialists can help to pinpoint underlying sleep issues, they're not a one-stop shop for solutions. Here I want to explore some complementary healthcare and wellness providers, perhaps less familiar to you, who can help your journey towards better sleep.

Who to see to...

Get you moving

If you've identified that a lack of balance in your physical fitness is playing a leading role in your sleep woes, then a physiotherapist could be just the healthcare provider you need.

While it might be tempting to jump straight in with a personal trainer or join the local boot camp, it's far better to do this in conjunction with a professional who is an expert in human movement and performance. That's where a physiotherapist can come in.

Physiotherapists are highly trained in the area of prevention, management and treatment of movement disorders. They see good movement as key to wellbeing and will help you gain, or regain, good posture, core strength and stability, and easeful mobility and flexibility. Your physiotherapist will work with you to identify your personal impediments to good movement and the opportunities you have for improving your physical fitness.

If you haven't been moving for a while or have ongoing unhealthy movement patterns, a physiotherapist will help you devise a program that will get you moving safely and effectively, and will recommend the best types of exercise for getting back into action. They will also work in conjunction with your doctor, your personal trainer or your sports coach to make sure everyone is on the same page when it comes to activity levels and safe movement patterns.

Overcome chronic pain

If chronic pain, ongoing headaches, issues with jaw clenching or frequent soft tissue ailments and injuries are impeding your ability to get quality sleep at night, an osteopath may well be the best fit for you. Osteopaths and physiotherapists overlap to a large degree, and differences often come down to the individual practitioner. However, osteopaths are generally more focused on manual therapies as part of their approach. Through their extensive training, osteopaths gain a highly developed sense of touch, which they use to examine, diagnose and treat all parts of the body – bones, joints, muscles and soft tissue. They can recognise issues within the circulatory, nervous and lymphatic systems of the body.

When you visit the osteopath you can expect a wide range of hands-on techniques in treatment, including stretching, massage, joint mobilisation and rehabilitation exercises. More specialised techniques, such as dry needling and electrotherapy, may also be recommended. Your osteopath will conduct a full osteopathic examination and, if necessary, clinical tests. This may involve diagnostic, orthopaedic or neurological tests, postural assessments and activities or exercises, which will help determine how best to manage your condition.

Up your nutrition game

If you're looking for someone to help you establish a higher-quality diet and reap the benefits of better nutrition for your weight, your vitality and your sleep quality, checking in with a nutritionist could be the best option for you.

A nutritionist will examine your weight, health and medical history and assess your current diet. Taking things like food intolerances, allergies, social factors and personal food preferences into consideration, they will help you set some nutrition goals and develop a game plan to get you there. Many of them offer ongoing coaching and contact between visits in order to help you establish new habits and feel supported and accountable as you tweak your diet.

Beat systemic stress

If you're sensing that a broader diagnosis of 'stress' is what is impeding your sleep, then consider booking in with a chiropractor. When it comes to help with sleeping problems, a well-trained chiropractor will be able to help you identify and manage stressors, whether physical or otherwise, that are contributing to nervous system overload.

When you think of chiropractic, your mind probably goes immediately to 'back pain' or 'spine adjustments'. And it's true – chiropractors focus largely on the spine. Your chiropractor will be on the lookout for 'vertebral subluxation', which is when a spinal bone misaligns, causing interference to the nervous system and nerve irritation. So if you've got postural and pain issues, a chiropractor is another option, alongside the physiotherapist and the osteopath.

Yet chiropractic doesn't just focus on musculoskeletal disorders. The basis of chiropractic practice is the belief that the spine has direct neurological influence on the rest of the body. The aim of care and treatment is to allow better communication throughout the body, especially between the spine and the brain, also called the central nervous system.

However, adjustments to the spine are just one way in which your chiropractor will work to improve your wellbeing. Chiropractors believe that the body has an innate ability to heal itself once stressors are removed. Practitioners focus on identifying obstacles and interferences that could be impeding your health, such as poor posture, poor nutrition, physical and emotional stress and muscular tension and tightness. Many practitioners have broadened their skill sets to include nutritional therapies, stress management techniques and herbal supplementations.

Bring life into focus

Maybe you've identified that your sleep is disturbed for more existential reasons. You're feeling a bit stuck in your work, or you're lacking direction in relationships, or your mindset is not as positive as you want it to be and you're not sure where to start.

If you have a specific trauma to work through or an existing mental health condition that needs attention, then finding a psychologist or counsellor could be the appropriate way forward for you. But if your issues are more general, consider a life coach.

A life coach won't spend a great deal of time nosing around in the murky waters of your past. Instead, they'll start with where you're at now, help you identify where you want to be, and help you close the gap between them.

Life coaches are skilled at helping you figure out what stories you're telling yourself and whether these are serving you. Working with a life coach, you'll be able to more quickly identify and change limiting beliefs and set meaningful goals in any area of your life.

All of this may feel tangential to sleep, but if it's the big life questions that are keeping you awake at night, or the underlying stories you're telling yourself that are holding you in patterns of sleep and health sabotage, a life coach may be exactly the right person to have on your dream team.

> **Exercise: Reflect on your life/sleep priorities**
>
> 1. **Think back over Part 2.** Which parts of your life could do with some clearer attention? Jot down a list of all the things you'd like to work on.
>
> 2. **Now number this list in order of priority.** Which item ranks as the top priority for making a positive change to your sleep quality?
>
> 3. **Now consider whether external support could benefit you in this area.** If so, which health professional might be the best person to check in with?

Choosing the right match for you

If you've narrowed down your modality, there's still the question of finding the right individual practitioner for you.

It's quite normal to make your decision about which practitioner to see based on pragmatic concerns: availability, proximity and cost. You base your decision on finding the nearest, most convenient practice, opt for the person who can fit you in soonest, or base your decision on fees and healthcare rebates.

Time and money are not insignificant concerns, and it's natural that they should come into play as you make decisions. If you're lucky, your nearest, most convenient practitioner will also turn out to be awesome.

But seeing as you will be investing time, money and even emotional energy in your healthcare visits, you have every right to be discerning about whether your practitioner will be everything you need.

What's more, there's evidence to show that the strength of the working alliance between you and your health provider is the make-or-break factor when it comes to how effective you find the treatment. If you find going to your see your chiropractor or physiotherapist an enjoyable, empowering experience, then you're actually going to experience their treatment as *more effective* than experiencing the same kind of care from a practitioner where there's not the same level of trust or rapport – because you'll be more likely to own and adopt their suggestions.[108]

Most of the time, we're only going to get a feel for whether we've got a good rapport with someone after a visit or two. Savvy practitioners know this, which is why some modalities offer free initial consults or 'get to know you' sessions. Take advantage of these if you find them, as you can't really know whether you're going to work well together until you've given it some time. However, don't feel obligated to return if you're not liking what you see.

What ingredients are necessary for a good working alliance? When searching for the right fit for you, consider the following traits.

1. They take the 'coach' approach

First and foremost, you want a practitioner who coaches, not someone who commands change. You want someone who will teach you how to take charge of your own health, not someone who is going to attempt to take charge of it for you.

We've all been to that doctor who acts like a kindly dictator, smiling while chastising us for our poor life choices and asking us to try a bit harder. Some of us even get drawn to the taskmaster types, thinking that we need harsh external rules imposed in order to get anything done. But if we're complying out of fear or obligation, the changes won't stick.

A practitioner who coaches you won't dictate. They know you need to be self-motivated, not externally motivated, in order to see lasting change. Instead of demanding your adherence, a coach will use education and empowering techniques in order to demonstrate the benefits of adhering to their plan, heeding advice or cooperating with treatment. This approach will be far more likely to break through any resistance you have and win over your subconscious mind than a dictatorial person who tries to motivate with shame, guilt or a 'father knows best' approach.

Does your practitioner welcome questions and offer ongoing explanations? Do they seek to educate you and not just treat you? Do they encourage you to actively participate in your own health goals?

2. They demonstrate trustworthiness

To work well with someone you need to know, like and trust them. This goes for your mechanic, your accountant and your health professional. Getting to know and like someone is a personal thing – often you just click, or can sense the potential for good rapport early. Figuring out whether you can trust someone is also a gut instinct, but there are a few areas that demonstrate someone's trustworthiness more objectively.

Trustworthiness is shown first and foremost in the small things, like punctuality. If a practitioner constantly runs late, this is a red flag. It could mean that they're overbooking their practice or it could be a personal issue. Either way, keeping you waiting on a regular basis shows a lack of respect for you and your time.

Another red flag is if you feel like you're being rushed through your session. I once saw a health professional who kept glancing at the clock and yawning during our time together. It made me feel terrible, as though I was keeping him waiting. Needless to say, that alliance didn't last.

A trustworthy practitioner will also be transparent about how they work. They'll be open about expected visit length and frequency. They'll be clear about fees and charges. They will welcome questions about the efficacy and necessity of recommended treatments and will be willing to discuss alternatives with you. A trustworthy practitioner certainly won't use pressure tactics or try to upsell you on programs, products or procedures. If they have suggestions for you, they'll give you clear information and let you make your own choices.

3. They lead by example

Finally, look for a practitioner who leads by example. Whatever issues you're seeking to address and modality you are drawn to, your practitioner should be someone who walks the talk.

Are you asking your practitioner to be perfect? Should you be judging a book by its cover? No. But you want enough evidence that they practise what they preach to make their own practice plausible. Would you use a mechanic whose own car blows black smoke out the exhaust? Would you get tennis lessons from someone who is too unfit to move around the court?

Does your health coach show you, as well as tell you, what it looks like to move well, to eat well, to manage stress and pressure well?

More generally, does this person inspire you to be a better you? When I look to anyone as a coach, I look for people who embody the personal traits that I'd like to emulate. I always work best with people I aspire to be like. For me, that is someone who's really fit and healthy, who is very loving and caring, and who has great personal and family relationships and a healthy spiritual side. That's my vision and it's what I seek out in others. Think about your own vision and the traits you would like to emulate in others, both in their area of specialty and in who they are as people. Given that you're seeking help to get better sleep, it's important to find out about your practitioner's sleep philosophy and quality. Are they going to be a good example to you in this area?

Looking for these traits in your practitioner will help you find the right fit. But is it possible to know in advance whether a prospective health provider will have them? Here are some options:

- Check out the practice website if there is one, and read up about their philosophy of care and treatment methods.
- Look for testimonials or positive feedback by searching for the practitioner online.
- If you've been referred by a friend, ask their opinion about the practitioner's style, manner and character before you start.
- Ring the practice office and ask questions about times and costs, visit frequency, what ongoing care looks like and what you can expect during your first session.

Doing these things will help you move beyond the 'cheap and convenient' matrix to find that great healthcare coach who will support your goals.

I personally rely on a wide team of people from both personal and professional contexts to keep me motivated and accountable. At this point in my life, the things most likely to keep me awake are big-picture questions about life direction, business direction and relationship direction. Therefore, my main health coach currently is my life coach. He shows me how to lead myself well and listen to my heart, which in turn helps me to sleep soundly, and everything else flows from there. But in writing this book, I've realised I have more to learn about physical fitness and nutritional health. I'll be honest – I've dabbled in these areas, but they are not things I've mastered. I can see that it's time for me to get some more people on my team to help me commit to patterns that will help me thrive, not just survive.

Taking charge of your team

So a good health coach is going to be like a good mechanic – but don't lose sight of the fact that it's your car and you're in the driver's seat.

Let me tell you the story of my friend Amy.

Amy was in her mid-thirties and struggling with sleep deprivation. She had young kids who sometimes woke in the night, but even when they were sleeping well she found it hard to wind down. She often took a few hours to get to sleep, then woke several times overnight, feeling hot and restless. Sometimes she would go through 3am waking spells and not be able to get back to sleep, finally drifting off just before her husband's 6am alarm. She propped herself up in the day with multiple coffees.

What's more, Amy was feeling average all around. Her weight had crept up over five years and she was now in the obese category on the BMI chart, with more of that weight sitting around her belly than she was used to. Amy also struggled with mild depression and anxiety, and found herself drinking more heavily and eating for comfort when stressful events occurred around her.

Amy was sent for a sleep study with suspected sleep apnea. The study showed that, along with some occasional anxiety-related insomnia, Amy's sleep quality was poor: she had frequent microarousals that prevented her from entering deep, reparative sleep.

The sleep clinic took a three-pronged approach to sleep problems, categorising them as either physical (sleep apnea), psychological (insomnia) or neurological (due to brain chemistry). Amy had a bit of all three, but the specialist determined that her main issue was neurological. The only approach he offered for this was to try a specific medication to alter the brainwave patterns. Amy was reluctant, as this would mean taking a pill (which had its own side effects) for the rest of her life.

At this point, Amy opted out and decided to see what she herself could do to turn her sleep quantity and quality around. Her first decision was to see a psychologist to help with low-lying anxiety. She also decided her lack of activity could be contributing to the weight, so started with a personal trainer to establish an exercise routine. They worked on strength training together, and Amy added some more walking to her lifestyle. The personal trainer sent her off to a physiotherapist to work on some mobility issues and an old shoulder injury that was holding her back. The physiotherapist worked with Amy's trainer to build a great rehabilitation routine, and also encouraged Amy to shift her sleep posture from stomach to side sleeping

On the sleep front, things began to gradually improve. Amy noticed that exercising more helped her fall asleep more quickly at night, and this encouraged her to add more sessions to her week. She wore a step tracker during the day, and used it to monitor her sleep at night too – although after a while she realised this just made her anxious, so she turned that off and tuned in to how she was feeling instead. Amy and her husband also recognised that watching movies in bed together was not helping their sleep, so they switched to reading together in bed and kept movies for the lounge room.

As sleep improved, Amy noticed that her appetite began to regulate itself better. Her weight didn't change significantly for the first year, but her shape started changing and her midriff trimmed down. At this point, she consulted a nutritionist to see what more could be done to shift her weight, and received some helpful advice about how to balance her meals throughout the day for better energy. Amy found that eating more protein and getting more vegetables helped to ease her mid-afternoon grazing habits and sweet tooth, although she kept her favourite treat foods in the mix. After another eighteen months of consistent training and more nutritious eating, Amy had lost 15kg and was back into a healthy weight range.

A few years on and Amy's sleep is in a great place. She's not sure how much deep sleep she gets in comparison to her sleep test, but the changes to her anxiety levels and her physical health speak volumes. She and her husband enjoy their reading ritual at night, and both wake early to get some movement in before the day begins with the kids. She no longer feels anxious about her sleep quality and she drifts off easily most nights. Sometimes her kids still wake her up, but she returns to sleep more easily these days. When she has a bad night (because life happens) she gets up at the usual time and goes for a run or a work-out, but doesn't push herself too hard. She told me she just loves the routine of being up early now, and knows how important that early morning start is to her whole mindset for the day.

I think a story like Amy's goes to show that fixing up your sleep and building a healthy lifestyle is never going to be about a quick fix. It takes time. It takes a team. But whatever supports you gather around you, don't forget this one thing: you're the one in charge.

CONCLUSION

I wrote this book based on two convictions. First, that good sleep is hands down the most helpful, useful, accessible tool we have to help us survive and thrive amid the stressors of modern life. And second, that regardless of how poor our sleep currently is, we all have what it takes to reconnect with our natural capacity to sleep soundly and to let the benefits of great sleep bring healing and energy and positivity into our lives.

I hope that by journeying through the world of sleep with me, you now share this conviction. Now you've reached the end of this book, you:

- Understand the relationship between good sleep and thriving in all spheres of life,
- Have insight into how sleep affects your thinking, working, moving, eating and loving – and vice versa,
- Know where the pressure points are for you and what to do about them, and
- Are ready to set up your own sleep environment, routine and healthcare team.

Bringing this all together, you have the tools to create the positive sleep spiral that can bring health and vitality to your life.

Now it's up to you to get started.

At this point, it's easy to get stuck. You could make one of two common mistakes.

If you're an enthusiastic change maker, you might try to jump in, boots and all, to a whole new approach to sleep. You'll audit your work stress, overhaul your exercise and eating regimens, take on six new visualisation and meditation techniques and drag your partner into revamping your sleep set-up – simultaneously. You'll go-all out trying to be the best damn sleeper you can be, and you may just burn out in the process.

If you're a more cautious type, then you're likely to get stuck deciding which move to make first. You'll decide on making a change but then worry if you're doing it out of sequence. You'll spend ages trying to decide whose help to ask for and which habits to adopt. You're worried about doing it wrong and you may never get started for fear of failure.

To both types of people, I say this: forget perfection and start small. Choose the topic that resonated most with you and begin with that. Which topic sticks most in your mind? Flick back to that chapter and find one thing that you want to work on: one habit you'd like to put in place; one conversation you'd like to have; one new way of thinking you'd like to try. *Just one thing.*

If you're still not sure, do this visualisation exercise.

Twelve months from now, you and I bump into each other at a café. We've never met, but you recognise me from my author picture at the back of this book and we strike up a conversation. You tell me, 'Tim, since reading your book I am getting the best sleep of my life.' I say, 'Wow, I'm so happy to hear that. Can you tell me more about how you're feeling?' You say, 'I'm calmer, I'm happier and I'm so much healthier than I was a year ago.' You tell me about all the things that have improved – how you're enjoying your work and relationships more, or how you're in better physical shape, or how you're getting up at the same time every morning and enjoying the new sense of purpose and focus in your day.

You tell me in great detail about where you used to be at and where you are at now. I'm really inspired by your story and the energy and enthusiasm you have. So I ask you, 'What did you have to do to get from that place you were in to where you are now? Where did you start?'

The answer you give me in this imagined scene will tell you where it is you need to get started on your path to great sleep.

Wherever you decide to start, and no matter how small your first step, you are setting your positive sleep spiral in motion. As the changes begin to take root, the next steps will become apparent to you. Trust yourself and enjoy the process. And if you ever get stuck – just sleep on it.

ABOUT THE AUTHOR

Tim joined Regal Sleep Solutions in 2012, bringing more than ten years of experience in sales and marketing. His educational background in journalism, film and television sharpened his creativity and developed his curiosity for the health sector. Tim first demonstrated his flair for sales in two years of work in film PR and on film sets in London. Following that, he spent seven years in the sports advertising industry, where he ranked in the top four marketers for sports advertising nationally.

Tim's passion for supporting clients' health with quality mattress and bedding products is rooted in his family, who have owned Regal, a leading mattress business, for more than thirty years. Within three years at the company, Tim fostered relationships with more than 2,000 health professionals across Melbourne.

Tim works with these health professionals to develop high-end mattresses, beds, and bedding products sold at factory-direct prices, thanks to Regal's dual role as manufacturer and retailer. Tim also developed Regal's signature Healthy Life Program in partnership with his father, Rob Simon, and postural expert Dr Michael Haworth.

ABOUT THE CREATE A DREAM FOUNDATION

The Create a Dream Foundation works like a 'make a wish' foundation for adults suffering terminal illnesses, forming magic moments that inspire joy and spark hope in the midst of a person's darkest challenge.

Our purpose is to positively touch the lives of those who feel marginalised while suffering terminal disease, when people need love and support more than ever. We believe that through love, care and dream fulfilment we will dramatically improve such people's lives.

The Create a Dream Foundation was developed in honour of Janine Kirzner and Elizabeth Simon, who both had their lives cut short by cancer. You can read more about them below.

All proceeds from this book will go to the Foundation.

For further information, please contact Tim Simon at:

Regal Sleep Solutions Head Office
1/800 Princes Hwy
Springvale, Vic. 3171
P: +61 3 9795 6300

The beginning of Create a Dream

I still remember the day my mum, Elizabeth, was diagnosed with cancer. I came home to our family house in Brisbane and she told me she had something to tell me. We went for a walk together with our beautiful golden Labrador, Arthur, and she told me the news that she'd been diagnosed with lung cancer and had six months to live.

My whole world stopped. Everything that I thought was important came tumbling down. But Mum looked me in the eye and said, 'I'm going to beat this. I've got this.' Mum did all the right things – the nutrition, the exercise – and because of her attitude and take on life she managed to extend her time with us to three years.

One of the magnificent things my mum did in that time was to dedicate herself to supporting and advocating for people who had received a lung cancer diagnosis yet had never smoked. She saw how this group was marginalised during the hardest time of their lives, and wanted to provide support and care instead.

A few years later my step-mum, Janine, who was also a true mother to me and central to my family, was diagnosed with lung cancer. Janine took the opposite approach to my mum and decided she was going to maintain her current lifestyle and 'go out without a fuss'. Within three months of diagnosis, Janine had left us.

Through my experience of losing both of these amazing women, I grew passionate about supporting adults with cancer. So many people are judged harshly for their diagnosis and made to feel ashamed and unsupported at precisely the time they need the most care and support. No one who gets sick with cancer, whether it is potentially related to lifestyle or seems to be random, deserves to be stigmatised or marginalised because of their diagnosis. They are still someone's mother, father, friend or child – they still mean something to other people.

This is why I established the Create a Dream Foundation. I want to bring a bit of joy, love and happiness back to those with terminal illness, as best I can.

ACKNOWLEDGEMENTS

I'd like to thank the following people, who have been behind me all the way in writing this book.

Wayne Todd – You're an inspiration, a great friend and someone I always connect deeply with. I look at how you are with your family connection, and it's something to aspire to.

Jason Smith – I have a man crush on you! What you've achieved in business is remarkable and I've modelled a lot of my own business on what you've done. Every chance to talk to you is a treat.

Damien Kristof – To watch our businesses grow simultaneously has been really rewarding and I've really enjoyed going down the growth path with you. Thank you for all your care and support.

Mike Haworth – You've been there since the beginning of my health journey. Nothing has ever been too hard for you. You've always been there and I really appreciate that you've got my back (literally as well as figuratively!).

Peter Dickens – You're the Yin to my Yang. Without you I would be unbalanced; thank you for always being a calming presence for me.

Julian Kirzner – You're a great mentor. You tell me when I mess up and you're just as quick to pat me on the back when I do right. We've ridden the rollercoaster of life together –although not by blood, you are a true brother.

Ben Carvosso – You got my inner compass working again. Without you I'd go off course.

The Regal family – I value every one of you. You're all unique and special, and you give your most valuable resource to me daily – your time. Thank you for this gift.

The Regal health professional network – You know who you are. You are the lifeblood of our organisation. Without you, we would not exist.

Carol from Foamco – Because of your support and belief in this project we now have this book. Without you this information may never have been shared. Thank you.

Simon Cowan – You're loyal as the day is long. Your expertise in manufacturing has made Regal what it is today.

Gina, my editor – Thanks for making me sound so much smarter than I am. Your research, dedication and the time you've put into this project is more than I could imagine. I am blessed to have met you.

Chelse, Tom, James, Rowe, Ev and Anthony – Mates for life. You've been there for me during good times and bad. You're my dearest friends in the world.

Rob Simon – I'm honoured to get to play with your train set. I've learnt so much from the opportunities you've given me. I've never met a man with more integrity, optimism and generosity. I'm honoured to be your son and proud that you're my father.

Phil Turner – Thank you for being able to read the instruments on the family plane. Without you we'd no doubt crash into a mountain.

Janine Kirzner – You were the strict mum I always needed and balanced our family out perfectly. Without you the family would have fallen apart. You are missed, but are in our hearts every day.

Elizabeth Simon (Mum) – I dedicate this book to you. You were always pissed off that I didn't read when I was younger, especially because you owned a bookstore and couldn't work out where you went wrong. Now that I've matured, I can celebrate your life, your contribution and the love you've shared on this planet in this book.

Juliana – I didn't know that someone could make me so happy and fill me with so much love. I hope I do the same for you. I strive for that daily.

NOTES

Introduction

1. Julie Power, 'Restless Nights and Zombie Days: Sleep Anxiety Is the New Zeitgeist', *Sydney Morning Herald*, 10 June 2016, smh.com.au/national/restless-nights-and-zombie-days-sleep-anxiety-is-the-new-zeitgeist-20160610-gpg9nb.html.
2. DR Hillman and LC Lack, 'Public Health Implications of Sleep Loss: the Community Burden', *Medical Journal of Australia* 199/8 (October 2013): 7–10.
3. Ibid.
4. Kim Arlington, 'Why Australians Aren't Getting Enough Sleep', 4 January 2017, smh.com.au/lifestyle/health-and-wellbeing/waking-up-is-hard-to-do-why-australians-arent-getting-enough-sleep-20161201-gt1k9y.html.
5. 'Too Wired for Sleep', *The Age* (multimedia website), http://www.theage.com.au/multimedia/toowiredforsleep/main.html.

1. The Problem

6. Shawn Kelly, 'A History of Sleep Remedies', *Sydney Morning Herald*, 30 December 2008, accessed 30 August 2017, http://ezinearticles.com/?History-of-Sleep-Remedies&id=1831664.
7. 'Why Do We Sleep, Anyway?' Division of Sleep Medicine at Harvard Medical School, last modified 18 December 2007, http://healthysleep.med.harvard.edu/healthy/matters/benefits-of-sleep/why-do-we-sleep.
8. 'The Learning Process and Sleep', Division of Sleep Medicine at Harvard Medical School, last modified 18 December 2007, http://healthysleep.med.harvard.edu/healthy/matters/benefits-of-sleep/learning-memory.
9. W Chris Winter, *The Sleep Solution: Why Your Sleep Is Broken and How to Fix It* (London: Scribe, 2017), 12.
10. Wayne Todd, *SD Protocol: Achieve Greater Health by Learning to Balance Your Physical, Chemical and Emotional Wellbeing*, (Sale: Clare McIvor, 2015). Dr Wayne Todd's book goes into great depth on this subject and provides a unique protocol for managing and eliminating stressors for better health.

11. 'Consumer Products', American Chemical Society, last modified 29 August 2014, https://www.acs.org/content/acs/en/education/whatischemistry/landmarks/newproducts.html.

12. 'Development of Tide Synthetic Detergent', American Chemical Society, last modified 20 November 2015, https://www.acs.org/content/acs/en/education/whatischemistry/landmarks/tidedetergent.html#p-and-g-synthetic-detergents.

13. Wayne Todd, *Insomnia: Where Does it Start?*, PDF ebook, http://www.sdprotocol.com.au/ebook-downloads-sd.

14. Karine Spiegel, Kristen Knutson, Rachel Leproult, Esra Tasali and Eve Van Cauter, 'Sleep Loss: A Novel Risk Factor for Insulin Resistance and Type 2 Diabetes', *Journal of Applied Physiology* vol. 99 no. 5 (November 2005): 2008–2019.

15. Winter, *The Sleep Solution*, 12.

16. Anna Patty, 'Lack of Sleep Is Costing the Economy More than $66 Billion', *The Age*, 8 August 2017 http://www.theage.com.au/business/workplace-relations/lack-of-sleep-is-costs-the-economy-more-than-66-million-20170807-gxqrew.html.

17. Matthew J Belvedere, 'Why Aetnas CEO Pays Workers up to $500 to Sleep', CNBC, 5 April 2016, cnbc.com/2016/04/05/why-aetnas-ceo-pays-workers-up-to-500-to-sleep.html.

18. 'Too Wired for Sleep', *The Age* (multimedia website), http://www.theage.com.au/multimedia/toowiredforsleep/main.html.

2. The Solution

19. Kirk Miller et al., 'Health Status, Health Conditions, and Health Behaviors among Amish Women: Results from the Central Pennsylvania Women's Health Study', *Women's Health Issues* 17/3 (2007): 162–171.

20. Diego Robles Mazzotti et al., 'Human Longevity Is Associated with Regular Sleep Patterns, Maintenance of Slow Wave Sleep, and Favorable Lipid Profile', *Frontiers in Aging Neuroscience* 6 (2014): 134, Abstract, https://www.ncbi.nlm.nih.gov/pmc/articles/PMC4067693/.

21. J Axelsson et al., 'Beauty Sleep: Experimental Study on the Perceived Health and Attractiveness of Sleep Deprived People', *British Medical Journal* 341 (2010): 1287–1289.

22. Press release, nobelprize.org, 2 October 2017, https://www.nobelprize.org/nobel_prizes/medicine/laureates/2017/press.html.

23. Press release, nobelprize.org, 2 October 2017, https://www.nobelprize.org/nobel_prizes/medicine/laureates/2017/press.html.
24. Camilla Kring, 'Chronobiology', B-Society, http://www.b-society.org/research.
25. Stephanie Hegarty, 'The Myth of the Eight-Hour Sleep', BBC World Service, 22 February 2012, http://www.bbc.com/news/magazine-16964783.
26. Max Hirchkowitz et al., 'National Sleep Foundation's Sleep Time Duration Recommendations: Methodology and Results Summary', *Sleep Health Journal* 1/1 (2015): 40–43, http://www.sleephealthjournal.org/article/S2352-7218%2815%2900015-7/fulltext.
27. Winter, *The Sleep Solution*, 31.
28. Allsion G Harvey and Nicole Tang, '(Mis)Perception of Sleep in Insomnia: A Puzzle and Resolution', *Psychology Bulletin* 138/1 (January 2012): 77–101.
29. Winter, *The Sleep Solution*, 85.
30. Kathrine Russo et al., 'Consumer Sleep Monitors: Is There a Baby in the Bathwater?' *Nature and Science of Sleep* vol. 7 (2015): 147–157, Abstract, https://www.ncbi.nlm.nih.gov/pmc/articles/PMC4640400/.

3. Thinking Well: Forming a Healthy Sleep Mindset

31. Erik M Gregory and Pamela B Rutledge, *Exploring Positive Psychology: The Science of Happiness and Well-Being* (California: Greenwood, 2016).
32. Jill McAbe, 'How to Turn Your New Year's Resolution – and Every Goal – into Reality', *Thrive Global*, 6 January 2017, https://journal.thriveglobal.com/use-the-neuroscience-of-goal-setting-to-turn your-new-years-resolutions-into-realities-25f853aede5b.
33. Winter, *The Sleep Solution*, 128–130.
34. C M Morin, F Blais and J Savard, 'Are Changes in Beliefs and Attitudes about Sleep Related to Sleep Improvements in the Treatment of Insomnia?' *Behavior Research and Therapy* vol. 40/7 (July 2002): 741–752.
35. Mayo Clinic staff, 'Insomnia Treatment: Cognitive Behavioral Therapy Instead of Sleeping Pills', 28 September 2016, https://www.mayoclinic.org/diseases-conditions/insomnia/in-depth/insomnia-treatment/art-20046677.
36. The following material is a summary of chapter 7, 'How to change', from her book *You Can Heal Your Life*, (Carlsbad CA: Hay House Ltd, 1984).

4. Working Well: Mastering Work-Sleep Balance

37. Maria Popova, 'Thomas Edison, Power-Napper: The Great Inventor on Sleep and Success', 11 February 2013, https://www.brainpickings.org/2013/02/11/thomas-edison-on-sleep-and-success/.

38. Michael McGirr, *The Lost Art of Sleep*, (Sydney: Piccardor, 2009), 13.

39. Carol Connolly, Marian Ruderman and Jean Brittain Leslie, 'Sleep Well, Lead Well: How Better Sleep Can Improve Leadership, Boost Productivity, and Spark Innovation', white paper for the Center for Creative Leadership, April 2014, http://www.ccl.org/wp-content/uploads/2015/04/SleepWell.pdf.

40. Tony Crabbe, *Busy: How to Thrive in a World of Too Much* (London: Piatkus Books, 2014), 9.

41. Theo Merz, '"Nomophobia" Affects Majority of UK', *The Telegraph*, 27 August 2013, http://www.telegraph.co.uk/technology/news/10267574/Nomophobia-affects-majority-of-UK.html.

42. Tim Elmore, 'Nomophobia: A Rising Trend in Students', *Psychology Today*, 18 September 2014, https://www.psychologytoday.com/blog/artificial-maturity/201409/nomophobia-rising-trend-in-students.

43. Brett and Kate McKay, 'On the Seventh Day, We Unplug: How and Why to Take a Tech Sabbath', *Art of Manliness*, 20 May 2014, http://www.artofmanliness.com/2014/05/20/tech-sabbath/.

44. JC Quick, JD Quick, DL Nelson and JJ Hurrell, *Preventive Stress Management in Organizations* (Washington DC: American Psychological Association, 1997).

45. Lissa Rankin, *Mind Over Medicine: Scientific Proof that You Can Heal Yourself* (Carlsbad CA: Hay House, 2013), 106.

46. James Campbell Quick and Demetria F Henderson, 'Occupational Stress: Preventing Suffering, Enhancing Wellbeing', *International Journal of Environmental Research and Public Health* 13/6 (May 2016): 459.

47. 'Workplace Stress – General', Canadian Centre for Occupational Health and Safety, last modified 13 November 2017, http://www.ccohs.ca/oshanswers/psychosocial/stress.html.

48. Pia Schönfeld et al., 'The Effects of Daily Stress on Positive and Negative Mental Health: Mediation through Self-Efficacy', *International Journal of Clinical and Health Psychology* 16/1 (2016): 1–10.

49. 'We Reviewed Over 60 Studies about What Makes for a Dream Job. Here's What We Found', 80000 Hours, last modified April 2017, https://80000hours.org/career-guide/job-satisfaction/#dont-aim-for-low-stress.

50. Ibid.

5. Moving Well: The Sleep-Exercise Connection

51. Bryonie Scott and Nicki Russell, 'Peak Athletic Performance Depends on Athletes' Sleep Cycles, New Research Shows', *Sydney Morning Herald*, 2 February 2015, http://www.smh.com.au/technology/sci-tech/peak-athletic-performance-depends-on-individual-athletes-sleep-cycles-new-research-shows-20150202-133vd7.html.

52. Russell Jackson, 'Nick Littlehales: The Man Who Taught Cristiano Ronaldo How to Sleep', *The Guardian*, 23 July 2015, https://www.theguardian.com/football/blog/2015/jul/23/nick-littlehales-the-man-who-taught-cristiano-ronaldo-how-to-sleep; Danielle Elliot, 'The Doctor Who Coaches Athletes on Sleep', *The Atlantic*, 23 April 2014, https://www.theatlantic.com/health/archive/2014/04/for-better-performance-athletes-need-sleep/361042/.

53. Ariana Huffington, *The Sleep Revolution: Transforming Your Life, One Night at a Time* (London: WH Allen, 2016), 261.

54. CD Mah et al., 'The Effects of Sleep Extension on the Athletic Performance of Collegiate Basketball Players', *Sleep* 34/7 (July 2011): 943–950.

55. Check out Jason's book, *Get Yourself Back in Motion* (Melbourne: Global Publishing Group, 2012).

56. GS Passos, 'Effect of Acute Physical Exercise on Patients with Chronic Primary Insomnia', *Journal of Clinical Sleep Medicine* 6/3 (June 2010): 270–275.

57. Alice Park, 'The Benefits of Exercise Add up: Over Time, a Little Goes a Long Way', *Time Magazine*, 6 September 2011, http://healthland.time.com/2011/09/06/the-benefits-of-exercise-add-up-over-time-a-little-goes-a-long-way/.

58. Lee T Ferris et al., 'Resistance Training Improves Sleep Quality in Older Adults: A Pilot Study', *Journal of Sports Science Medicine* 4/3 (September 2005): 354–360.

59. Emma Wynne, 'When the Pursuit of Fitness and Exercise Is a Slog, How Do We Stay Motivated?' *ABC Radio*, 24 August 2017, http://www.abc.net.au/news/2017-08-24/tips-to-help-you-stay-motivated-to-exercise/8835084?sf108780192=1.

60. Ibid.

61. Thai Nguyen, 'Hacking into Your Happy Chemicals': Dopamine, Serotonin, Endorphins and Oxytocin', *Huffington Post*, 20 October 2014, blog, https://www.huffingtonpost.com/thai-nguyen/hacking-into-your-happy-c_b_6007660.html. Simon Sinek gives a cool explanation of these hormones in his TED talk based on his most recent book, *Leaders Eat Last* (London: Penguin, 2017). See https://www.ted.com/speakers/simon_sinek.

62. 'For Best Sleep, Work Up a Sweat in the Morning', American College of Sports Medicine, last modified 2017, http://www.acsm.org/about-acsm/media-room/acsm-in-the-news/2011/08/01/for-best-sleep-work-up-a-sweat-in-the-morning.

63. William W Deardorff, 'Chronic Pain and Insomnia: Breaking the Cycle', *Spine Health*, 12 December 2016, https://www.spine-health.com/wellness/sleep/chronic-pain-and-insomnia-breaking-cycle.

64. Esther Han, 'Prescription Opioids Are Killing More Australians than Heroin', *Sydney Morning Herald*, 24 July 2017, http://www.smh.com.au/national/health/prescription-opioids-are-killing-more-australians-than-heroin-australian-bureau-of-statistics-20170720-gxf5wa.html.

65. For some amazing stories that help explain pain biology, read Lorimer Moseley's *Painful Yarns* (Adelaide: Noigroup, 2007).

66. Maureen C Jensen et al., 'Magnetic Resonance Imaging of the Lumbar Spine in People without Back Pain', *New England Journal of Medicine* 331 (1994): 69–73.

67. GL Moseley, 'Evidence for a Direct Relationship Between Cognitive and Physical Change During an Education Intervention in People with Chronic Low Back Pain', *European Journal of Pain* 8 (2004): 39–45.

68. Michael C Hsu et al., 'Sustained Pain Reduction through Affective Self-Awareness in Fibromyalgia: a Randomized Controlled Trial', *Journal of General Internal Medicine* 25/10 (October 2010): 1064–1070, https://www.ncbi.nlm.nih.gov/pmc/articles/PMC2955480/.

6. Eating Well: The Key Ingredients for a Good Night's Sleep

69. Adam Hadhazy, 'Think Twice: How the Gut's "Second Brain" Influences Mood and Well-Being', *Scientific American*, 12 February 2010, https://www.scientificamerican.com/article/gut-second-brain/.

70. Siri Carpenter, 'That Gut Feeling', *Monitor on Psychology* 43/8 (September 2012): 50, http://www.apa.org/monitor/2012/09/gut-feeling.aspx.

71. Felice N Jacka et al., 'Association of Western and Traditional Diets with Depression and Anxiety in Women', *American Journal of Psychiatry* 167/3 (2010): 305–311.

72. http://www.who.int/foodsafety/faq/en/.

73. Carmel Harrington, *The Complete Guide to a Good Night's Sleep* (Melbourne: Macmillan, 2014), Kindle edition, ch. 16.

74. Joel J Heidelbaugh, 'Proton Pump Inhibitors and Risk of Vitamin and Mineral Deficiency: Evidence and Clinical Implications', *Therapeutic Advances in Drug Safety* 4/3 (June 2013): 125–133.

75. Gregory D M Potter, Janet E Cade and Laura J Hardie, 'Longer Sleep Is Associated with Lower BMI and Favorable Metabolic Profiles in UK adults: Findings from the National Diet and Nutrition Survey', *PLOS ONE* 12/7 (2017), http://journals.plos.org/plosone/article?id=10.1371/journal.pone.0182195.

76. Lisa M Nackers et al., 'The Association Between Rate of Initial Weight Loss and Long-Term Success in Obesity Treatment: Does Slow and Steady Win the Race?', *International Journal of Behavioural Medicine* 17/3 (September 2010 Sep): 161–167.

7. Loving well: The Art of Sleeping Together

77. Tina Sundelin, Mats Lekander, Kimmo Sorjonen and John Axelsson, 'Negative Effects of Restricted Sleep on Facial Appearance and Social Appeal', *Royal Society Open Science* 4 (April 2017), http://rsos.royalsocietypublishing.org/content/4/5/160918.

78. Wendy M Troxel et al., 'Marital Quality and the Marital Bed: Examining the Covariation between Relationship Quality and Sleep', *Sleep Medicine Review* 11/5 (October 2007): 309–404, https://www.ncbi.nlm.nih.gov/pmc/articles/PMC2644899/.

79. James M Parish, 'The Pursuit of Happiness: Sleep Apnea, Sex, and Sleepiness', *Journal of Clinical Sleep Medicine* 6/3 (June 2010): 227–228, https://www.ncbi.nlm.nih.gov/pmc/articles/PMC2883032/.

80. 'Snoring and Hypnosis', Tracey Gordon Hypnotherapy, 15 June 2015, http://www.sleephypnosis.co.nz/snoring-and-hypnosis/.

81. David Kraft, 'Successful Treatment of Snoring Using Hypnosis', *Contemporary Hypnosis and Integrative Therapy* 30 (2015): 179–188.

82. Judith L Reishtein et al., 'Outcome of CPAP Treatment on Intimate and Sexual Relationships in Men with Obstructive Sleep Apnea', *Journal of Clinical Sleep Medicine* 6/3 (June 2010): 221–226, https://www.ncbi.nlm.nih.gov/pmc/articles/PMC2883031/.

83. Theresa E DiDonato, 'Why Your Relationship Depends on a Good Night's Sleep', *Psychology today*, 25 April 2014, https://www.psychologytoday.com/blog/meet-catch-and-keep/201404/why-your-relationship-depends-good-nights-sleep.

84. HE Gunn et al., 'Sleep Concordance in Couples is Associated with Relationship Characteristics.' *Sleep* 38/6 (June 2015): 933–939.

85. James Hamblin, 'Why Morning People Thrive', *The Atlantic*, 4 November 2016, https://www.theatlantic.com/health/archive/2016/11/if-your-child-is-terrible-blame-his-chronotype/506372/.

86. Kenneth P Wright Jr et al., 'Entrainment of the Human Circadian Clock to the Natural Light-Dark Cycle' *Current Biology* 23/16 (August 2013): 1554–1558.

87. Ibid.

88. Ruth Ostrow, 'The Sleep Divorce of Having Separate Bedrooms', *The Australian*, 31 March 2017, http://www.theaustralian.com.au/life/health-wellbeing/the-sleep-divorce-of-having-separate-bedrooms/news-story/a34a0de-6d2a0491c315671b6b9f6f49e.

89. Theresa E DiDonato, PhD, 'Why Your Relationship Depends on a Good Night's Sleep', *Psychology Today*, 25 April 2014, https://www.psychologytoday.com/blog/meet-catch-and-keep/201404/why-your-relationship-depends-good-nights-sleep.

90. Michael Breus, 'The Couple that Sleeps (Well) Together Stays Together', Share Care, https://www.sharecare.com/health/sex-and-relationships/article/the-couple-that-sleeps-well-together-stays-together.

91. American Academy of Sleep Medicine, 'Stable Marriage is Linked with Better Sleep in Women', AASM, 2 June 2009, https://aasm.org/stable-marriage-is-linked-with-better-sleep-in-women/.

92. AM Gordon, 'To Have and to Hold: Gratitude Promotes Relationship Maintenance in Intimate Bonds.' *Journal of Personal Social Psychology* 103/2 (August 2012): 257–274.

93. Gary Chapman, *The Five Love Languages: How to Express Heartfelt Commitment to Your Mate* (Chicago: Northfield, 1995).

94. A survey is available on the website http://www.5lovelanguages.com/.

8. Your Sanctuary

95. http://www.censusdata.abs.gov.au/census_services/getproduct/census/2016/quickstat/036.

96. By which I mean sex, of course. But in case you haven't heard, sleep is the new sex.

97. 'The secret to a good night's slumber is to sleep in a blue bedroom', Travelodge, 17 May 2013, https://www.travelodge.co.uk/press-centre/press-releases/SECRET-GOOD-NIGHT%E2%80%99S-SLUMBER-SLEEP-BLUE-BED-ROOM.

98. Andrea Downey, 'This is Why You Should Change Your Pillow Every Two Years', *The Sun*, 14 February 2017, https://www.thesun.co.uk/living/2863127/this-is-why-you-should-change-your-pillow-every-two-years-says-hygiene-doctor/.

9. Your Routine

99. Elise Facer-Childs and Roman Brandstaetter, 'The Impact of Circadian Phenotype and Time Since Awakening on Diurnal Performance in Athletes', *Current Biology Online* (January 2015), http://www.cell.com/current-biology/fulltext/S0960-9822(14)01639-X.

100. Sierra B. Forbrush et al., 'Sociodemographics, Poor Overall Health, Cardiovascular Disease, Depression, Fatigue, and Daytime Sleepiness Associated with Social Jetlag Independent of Sleep Duration and Insomnia', *Sleep*, Vol. 40, Abstract Supplement, 2017.

101. Winter, *The Sleep Solution*, 183–196.

102. Jocko Willink, *Discipline Equals Freedom: A Field manual*. (New York: St Martin's Press, 2017).

103. From a Facebook Live event, quoted in 'Business Insider', https://www.businessinsider.com/retired-navy-seal-commander-jocko-willink-morning-routine-2016-10#061ct25OALB1muIA.99.

104. Shantha MW Rajaratnam, Mark E Howard and Ronald R Grunstein, 'Sleep Loss and Circadian Disruption in Shift Work: Health Burden and Management', *Medical Journal of Australia* 199/8 (2013): 11–15.

105. N Buscemi et al., 'Melatonin for Treatment of Sleep Disorders: Summary', *Evidence Reports/Technology Assessments* 108 (Rockville MD: Agency for Healthcare Research and Quality, 2004), https://www.ncbi.nlm.nih.gov/books/NBK37431/.

106. Joel Wong and Joshua Brown, 'How Gratitude Changes You and Your Brain', *Greater Good Magazine* 6 (June 2017) https://greatergood.berkeley.edu/article/item/how_gratitude_changes_you_and_your_brain.

10. Your Dream Team

107. Atul Gawande, 'Personal Best', *The New Yorker*, 3 October 2011, http://www.newyorker.com/magazine/2011/10/03/personal-best.

108. MJ Leach, 'Rapport: A Key to Treatment Success', *Complementary Therapies in Clinical Practice* 11/4 (November 2005):262–265.

www.ingramcontent.com/pod-product-compliance
Lightning Source LLC
Chambersburg PA
CBHW071911290426
44110CB00013B/1351